A Mended
and Broken Heart

A Mended
and Broken Heart

· ·

The Life and Love of Francis of Assisi

Wendy Murray

A Member of the Perseus Books Group
New York

SICUT
MANIFESTUM EST
Super omnia desiderare debeamus habere Spiritum Domini et
sanctam eius operationem et orare semper ad eum puro corde et
habere humilitatem et patientiam in persecutione et infirmitate.

For Nancy

Contents

• • • • • • • • • • •

Author's Note

● ● ● ● ● ● ● ● ● ● ● ●

Francis, son of Pietro Bernadone of Assisi, was born in A.D. 1182 and died in 1226. He started the mendicant order referred to as the "lesser brothers," the Order of the Friars Minor (O.F.M.: Franciscans). He was canonized by the Catholic Church in 1228. The birth year of Clare, daughter of Sir Favorone of Assisi, is not known. She followed Francis in his vow of penance and introduced the second arm of the order known as the Second Order, or the Poor Clares (female). She died in 1253 and was canonized in 1255. Francis' mortal remains rest in the Basilica of San Francesco in Assisi, Italy. Clare's mortal remains rest in the Basilica of Santa Chiara, also in Assisi.

Preface

❋ ❋ ❋ ❋ ❋ ❋ ❋ ❋ ❋ ❋ ❋ ❋

"Both fairies and journalists are slaves to duty," the writer G. K. Chesterton remarked, and never was that statement truer than in the researching and writing of this book. For me, it has meant sitting in caves, standing on precipices, slogging through wheat fields, and squeezing through hidden passageways. To "get the interview" I've eaten meals in unheated homes in the dead of winter, sipping wine and whiskey by firelight; I've whispered in dimly lit libraries with elderly friars hunched over ancient manuscripts; I've spoken with nuns behind iron grills; and I've sung vespers in Latin. I've waited for appointments in church officials' private chapels, where on one occasion I sat on a kneeler while a nun prayed at the altar on the floor. I too sat on floors—in libraries—and also on stools and ladders, scouring stacks for something, anything. Writing this book has meant resurrecting the *qui quae quod* of classical Latin that I studied for three years as a sometimes-clueless high school student. And this only to discover that medieval Latin involves the loss of declension endings, the extended use of auxiliary verbs, and (as one linguist put it) "anarchy in uses of the subjunctive and indicative." It has meant studying documents in French, Portuguese, Italian, and (thank God) English. It has meant chatting with friars in cafés, chasing down tour guides on the streets of Assisi, climbing watchtowers of ancient fortresses, lowering myself on ladders into subterranean ancient Roman ruins below semi-ancient medieval ones, and being yelled at by an Italian film director. (No project in Italy is complete without having been yelled at by an Italian film director.) I wrote this book with my legs.

In chasing down the story of Saint Francis of Assisi, I spoke with hundreds of people—scholars, theologians, priests, friars, nuns, bishops, artists, lawyers, maids, scientists, historians, archaeologists, café owners, writers, professors, actors, and, yes, a movie director. They were Italians mostly. Others were Dutch, French, German, Irish, Scottish, Latino, Asian, and even American. Everyone I spoke with knew something of Francis, and often what one knew contradicted what another one knew. I adopted the principle *No one can tell you everything, but everyone can tell you something.* That something—that one thing I hadn't heard before—added a piece to the improbable picture of the life of Francis of Assisi that I submit in this book. It is a story of a complicated man, a true Italian among Italians, a poet, a warrior, a knight, a lover, a madman, and a saint. It is a story about human love by lovers of God—"both at once," as Chesterton said, "both thoroughly."

A knowledgeable Franciscan told me that if you don't understand Francis of Assisi as a mystery, then you have to
conclude he was mad. Another Franciscan told me he *was*
mad—but in a way that did not bind, that instead set him
free. Still another said, "He is an ocean." How does one approach a mystery? A madman? An ocean?

The task is daunting. Finding dates and documentation
relating to Francis is the heartbreak of serious researchers,
since most early texts about Francis were destroyed in the
decades following his death in deference to what was then
deemed the only "official" biography (to be discussed).

An archaeologist friend of mine applies principles in his
field research that require digging for evidence, finding it,
scrutinizing it, consolidating it, and interpreting it. When
speaking of his discoveries, he frequently says, "and so the
implication is. . . ." I have followed the parameters of the
archaeologist. Pieces of the story of Saint Francis do remain, and I have dug through them. These pieces include
an understanding of the setting of the story (that is, the
Middle Ages), the stage of its unfolding (the Italian peninsula generally and Assisi specifically), and the script as
written by early biographers in the century after Francis'
death, along with the writings of both Francis and Clare. I
have scrutinized, consolidated, and interpreted these
pieces in a way that has enabled me to capture at least a
slice of the story of the life of this astonishing figure. I have
asked reasonable questions. I have said to myself, "and so
the implication is. . . ."

When brought together in logical unity, the pieces of Francis' story have, to my mind, rendered a subtext to the larger narrative that has been generally dismissed among scholars and historians as sentimental, modern, and implausible—that is, that Francis of Assisi's unique and irrepressible relationship with the extraordinary Clare Favorone of Assisi was initially rooted in love. This love, in turn, evolved into mutual renunciation as each pursued their individual life as a penitent religious. This book asserts that their renounced physical love ultimately defined the inner landscape of their devotional lives.

In his biography of Saint Francis, Chesterton challenges this supposition, asserting that modern people cannot conceive that the relationship between Francis and Clare was at every point wholly pure and transcendent and beyond the flesh, because, says Chesterton, they—modern people—"want love."[1] In my way of seeing it, the modern thinker might have more difficultly imagining the possibility that these two individuals did indeed love each other, then renounced that love for higher obligations, and stayed true to their vows—though it broke their hearts. Skeptics of this possibility say that neither Francis nor Clare was sentimental and so would not have capitulated to love in the first place. To be sure, neither Francis nor Clare was sentimental. Therefore, it seems to me entirely logical that as their spiritual lives awakened, any amorous inclinations they may have entertained would have been renounced in deference to the higher call they were hearing. My research has compelled me to conclude that this scenario is indeed plausible and rational and warrants honest exploration. True love truly transformed so as to remain truly pure is virtue in its most heroic sense. To rob Francis and Clare of the integrity of this aspect of their religious vows shrivels their virtue and diminishes their humanness.

The official record is, of course, fragmented and full of irregularities. We must therefore abandon hope for clear answers. We must also dispel the notion that Francis' short vaulting career from Assisi's troubadour playboy to the town's most prodigious religious can be tracked chronologically. Certain points can be. Many cannot. It is beside the point. Francis didn't operate on a linear plane. He blew apart in every direction at once. It is the *core* of the person that is under discussion, the matter that became antimatter. The "matter" is Francis the man; the "antimatter" is Francis the saint. If we know him only as the man, then he might as well be known, to borrow from Chesterton, as the world's "one quite sincere democrat." If we know him only as the saint, then he is a ghost who inhabits a spirit world beyond the reach of ordinary people. If Francis was anything, he was real. He was hopelessly anchored to real life.

Chesterton notes elsewhere that dual forces pull a human being in opposing directions, one toward God and another toward the flesh, "both burning . . . both things at once and both things thoroughly."[2] This captures the force of the transaction that forged Francis the man (matter) into Francis the saint (antimatter). Antimatter comes from its core, the same mass with the opposite electric charge. How does one discern matter from antimatter? The scientist says, "Measure the electric charge!" Based upon the criteria noted above, the case will be made that the electric charge that ultimately propelled Francis' conversion was his love for Clare. The man, true Francis, was a complete man, aflame with love for life and flesh and also for spirit and God—both at once and both thoroughly. A transaction occurred. In spite of the man, she harnessed and changed him. The outcome was the saint.

To become a saint means being raised to the full honors of the altar. It involves intense scrutiny of the person's life, writings, reputation for holiness, and associated miracles. Canonization demands, among other things, "virtue to a heroic degree." And yet Francis' profligate early life was well known by those who knew him—and by just about everybody else in Assisi. He was widely remembered as a young stallion roaming the streets at night, leading the pack of Assisi's wild youth in parties and song. Francis himself never recoiled from recalling those years of folly. Even after his prolonged conversion, he fought inside himself the continual battle of the temptation of the flesh. When his life was nearing its end and rumors of canonization were afoot, he told his brothers: "Don't canonize me too quickly. I am perfectly capable of fathering a child."[3]

Regardless, the canonization took place in a hasty process and the written histories of the saint began.[4] A multiplicity of narratives emerged, crafted by a diverse company of biographers. Depending upon their respective agendas, some glossed over his well-known, pre-conversion, amorous behavior toward women. The portrait of the saint as the second Christ arose and flowered in the aftermath of his death. As the story evolved, the presence of Clare as an intimate companion devolved.[5]

If tracking Francis is difficult, finding extant documents about the life of Clare is an even more vexing and despairing proposition. "Not a few were destroyed; others disappeared," notes Franciscan scholar Paschal Robinson. "As far as dates go, only one—the date of her canonization—is given." No early source renders a verifiable year of Clare's birth. "Save for a few fragments of pious legend," Robinson concludes, "we are without any exact knowledge of the life of Saint Clare down to 1212."[6]

So the creation of the saint and the separation of his story from Clare's began with Francis' canonization in 1228, two years after his death. At the time, Francis' personal friend and one-time guardian of the order, Bishop Ugolino of Ostia, was seated as Pope Gregory IX. Gregory was facing ongoing antagonism from the Holy Roman Emperor Frederick II just when the Church was already weakened by internal bickering, turf wars, and corruption. Frederick had incited a rebellion in Rome against the papacy that had forced Gregory to take refuge in Spoleto, a town just south of Assisi. The pope addressed these challenges to his authority in many ways, but

I highlight only one of his strategies: the veneration of saints. It helped Gregory's cause to beatify this local champion.

Less than two years after Francis' death, during the spring of 1228, Gregory implemented plans for his canonization. He issued a letter granting indulgence to any who made a contribution toward the construction of a basilica where Francis' mortal remains would take their final rest. Assisi's western slope, the *collis inferni*, had been the common burial ground for thieves, murderers, and lepers, and Francis had requested burial there. Gregory secured the land within days of Frederick's rebellion in Rome, and he himself, not the Franciscans, initiated the canonization process. On July 16, 1228, Francis was confirmed a saint. He emerged then as he remains today—among the Catholic tradition's most popular saints, connected as he was to the poor and common people.

Pope Gregory commissioned Thomas of Celano, a follower of Francis, to write the first biography of Francis (called a legend). Published in 1229, the legend known as Celano's *First Life* "created a tempest," a leading Franciscan told me, because the biographer minced no words about Francis' troublesome youth and placed some blame on his parents, one of whom (his mother) was still living. In 1247 Celano published a rewrite, the *Second Life*, then called *Remembrances*. In this version, hinting of satire, Francis is transformed into a Christ prototype and his mother into the paragon of virtue. Other legends were also in the making in these years. All of them told of heretofore unheard of elements of Francis' saintly activities.

The small town of Assisi as it would have looked when Francis lived. The *collis inferni* ("hill of hell") to the left is where Francis requested to be buried. The Basilica of San Francesco exists there today. (By Francesco Providone, seventeenth century.)

In order to consolidate and organize these versions into a coherent presentation of the saint, in 1260 Pope Alexander IV commissioned Bonaventure, then minister general of the Franciscans, to write the one and only "official" biography of Saint Francis. Bonaventure, who had been elected minister general of the order in 1257,[7] set about a meticulous reordering and consolidating of the decisions and records of all previous ministers general, the result being the "definitive" biography of Francis, titled *The Major Life*. Though he was the first hagiographer who did not know Francis personally, Bonaventure was revered for his accomplishment by being designated "second founder" of the Franciscan Order. *The Major Life* smoothed inconsistencies in earlier legends and highlighted Francis' life only with episodes that emphasized his sanctity. Bonaventure's legend was approved in 1263. Three years later, in an unprecedented action, the general chapter of Paris (a gathering of representatives from the order worldwide) ordered all previous legends of Francis destroyed in deference to Bonaventure's.

Fortunately for historians and lovers of Francis, not all obeyed the decree. Rare copies of books and writings survived the purge, including Celano's *First* and *Second Life* (along with his *Treatise on Miracles*), liturgical texts, and some material thought to be from the hand of Francis' close companion Brother Leo.[8] Some writings were hidden and tucked away in walls, in the folds of dead peoples' robes, and in back pages of ancient volumes. Optimists still hope more unknown documents may yet emerge. In any case, by the end of the fourteenth century Francis of Assisi was firmly positioned as a "second Christ." But this was only after several rewrites, evolution of texts, and censorship of the earliest documents.

* * * * * * * * * * *

From the end of the fourteenth century until the mid-nineteenth century, the Franciscan movement was consumed with internal factionalism and the evolution of its respective branches. So examination of the life of Francis himself was limited to a few studies, and these were written, in part, in response to the ongoing debates between the fracturing parties.[9]

The discovery of Francis' mortal remains in 1818, as well as Clare's in 1850, brought to light new information and reinvigorated the study of both lives, spawning a new outpouring of original research. The renaissance of scrutiny and appropriation of newly discovered source material lent researchers more tools, enabling them to explore wider themes behind the story. While the light of new research has not compromised Francis' unchallenged standing among the most beloved of Catholic saints, the new research has nevertheless demanded that he continue to be confronted as "the most problematic."[10]

Scholarship about Francis flourished in the late nineteenth century and has not dissipated. The rigorous and painstaking work of contemporary scholars has rendered greater clarity in all the realms of Francis' story relating to setting (history), stage (local custom), and the script (various early sources). Paul Sabatier, a French Protestant, was the first scholar to probe vigorously the history of Francis outside constraints of Catholic authority. Sabatier scoured libraries all over Italy and uncovered heretofore unknown original documents buried in pages of medieval volumes. He undertook a meticulous comparison of texts to track the evolution of the story in light of the history and culture of the time. His pioneering biography, *Vie de S. François d'Assise*, came out (in French) in 1894.[11] It was an instant best seller. Protestants and Catholics alike hailed it as a pioneering magnum opus of scholarly examination of Francis—though the Catholic Church was destined to consign the work to the Index Libororum Prohibitorum, books not sanctioned by the pope.

Sabatier's book was followed closely by Arnaldo Fortini's weighty *Nova Vita di San Francesco d'Assisi* (1926), in which the author, Assisi's mayor for many years, grounded his research in civic archival material in Assisi.[12] Fortini noted: "They who are guided by sources to study the life and work of St. Francis of Assisi immediately notice the void which manifests itself in the narration of the early biographers. . . . [T]he gaps can be filled by the study of documents contemporary to that era. The archives of the City of Assisi offer us a conspicuous source of study on the epoch of the Saint. The greatest part of this material has remained unknown to scholars until now."[13]

An honest exploration of Francis' life demands scrutiny of all available sources that have arisen in the historical and cultural context. It is my close examination of this context and these sources that has enabled me to cobble together a picture of Clare's rightful place in Francis' life. My early chapters therefore build upon historical material gleaned from knowledge of the times—the setting and the stage. The later chapters examine how the life of Francis unfolded within this context, which, of necessity, demands interaction with early writings (delineated in detail in the notes). When all the pieces are laid out and considered in logical unity, footprints appear. These would belong to Clare.

Catholic tradition still upholds and defends the officially sanctioned biography written by Bonaventure in 1263. In it, Clare is honored in her own right for sanctity and devotion, but her role in Francis' life is diminished. When Bonaventure was commissioned to write his biography, the Church generally and Franciscans specifically were struggling for unity and stability. They needed their saints because saints kept faith alive in the hearts of the people. And saints must be heroically virtuous. Of the primary biographies, if Clare appears at all she is consigned to the background. Yet I believe that she was a clear and primary player in Francis' life and spiritual formation—both before and after his conversion—and that she remained so until the day he died.

● ● ● ● ● ● ● ● ● ● ●

I have tried to keep the body of the text unburdened with names and source titles. Citations, elaborations, and related information regarding source material can be found in the endnotes. The majority of the material from which I quote comes from original documents that remain within the realm of public domain. I have polished grammatical blemishes, made some portions more concise, and sometimes left out ellipses. All minor adjustments have remained true to and consistent with the original Latin. I have used secondary sources sparingly (these are listed in the selected bibliography at the back of the book). The exception is Arnaldo Fortini.

Fortini's book *Francis of Assisi*, abridged and translated into English by Helen Moak, has been indispensable.[14] I have drawn frequently upon his use of primary source material from Assisi's ancient civic archives that is otherwise unavailable to even the most vigilant researcher. "The mysticism of Francis unfolds against the dramatic, violent and vibrant background of a bloody world," Fortini said. Local history thus is the "prime matter of the great universal movement" that helped spawn Saint Francis.[15] In other words, one cannot understand the man without examining his context. Fortini's daughter, Gemma Fortini, an accomplished scholar in her own right, called her father an "impassioned researcher of ancient documents."[16] Arnaldo Fortini meticulously culled invaluable information from some six hundred previously unknown primary documents from Assisi's archives. Paul Sabatier wrote in a letter to him, "[Yours is] a work which makes you the author of a life of Saint Francis conceived in a totally new manner."[17] Fortini fills in critical gaps existing in the works of Francis' early biographers who neglected (Sabatier continues) "the essentially Assisian character of the Saint." In this regard I echo the sentiment expressed by Umberto Eco: "We are dwarfs, but dwarfs who stand on the shoulders of giants."

A few technical notes: I have used English translation of early sources, but have consulted the original Latin and in some cases Italian and Portuguese. I capitalize the "c" in the word "Church" to denote the significance of the Roman Catholic Church in the days in which our story unfolds, the Middle Ages. For the same reason, I also make use of the male pronoun when referring to God, gender sensitivities notwithstanding.

"Francis of Assisi is not a man who can be calmly observed," says the great scholar Jacques Dalarun. "He is a man who must be confronted, with sympathy and commitment." Dalarun urges us: "Never give up on the quest for the historical Francis."[18] Examining the life of Francis of Assisi and, of necessity, his relationship to Clare is like looking into a fog over a restless sea. A light shines somewhere, but it is best seen by fixing one's gaze a little beyond it—and even then one never really knows if the light is within reach. Available information is obscure and inconsistent, so the best one can hope for is to capture a little light through a dense fog. That is my hope for this book— that it will cast a faint light. A leading friar and outstanding scholar in Assisi, whom I consulted regularly, said of Francis by way of parting words to me: "Don't say we caught him." We haven't. But my fervent hope is that through this book he will have caught you.

Wendy Murray
Assisi, Italy, 2007

A man has as much knowledge as he executes.
—Francis of Assisi

CHAPTER
OΠE

Assisi's Son

There was in that land a terrible dragon, which came out of the sea and went into the city and killed many persons and ate them. And one day all the people of the city armed themselves, the people and the knights, and went out after that dragon. And the dragon was so terrible to look at that the people began to run away. And the knights, more than two thousand of them, also ran away. The king, in order to appease the fury of the dragon, ordered that a maiden be given to him and that the choice of the maiden be made by lot. It happened that the lot fell to the daughter of the king, who was the most beautiful maiden of the time. And the king, held by his duty to the people, wept bitterly. But since there was nothing he could do, he had his daughter dressed nobly, like a bride, with a crown on her head, like a queen. He pressed her to him, then with terrible sorrow and weeping he sent her to the island where the dragon that was to devour her could be found. Left alone, so adorned and so beautiful, she waited, trembling, for the dragon.

Then the blessed Giorgio appeared on his great horse. He was the handsomest young man to be found anywhere and wore beautifully decorated armor. He went to the princess, who was crying, and said to her: "Gentle maiden, why are you crying here all by yourself?" She replied, "O most noble young man, I am waiting for the dragon that is to devour me. I beg you in courtesy to go away at once, so that you do not have to die with me, because it is to me that this cruel fate has fallen." At this point the dragon came out of the water and hissed loudly and came toward her. Blessed Giorgio ran to meet him and gave him a blow with his lance that immediately knocked him down. Then he called the maiden and had her take off her girdle and put it on the neck of the dragon. Thus the young princess drew it along behind her, like a lamb, all the way to the city. All the people greatly marveled in seeing such courage and such wisdom in so young a knight.

The king could not express his joy, seeing that his daughter escaped from so cruel a death. When the dragon was before the king, blessed Giorgio killed it, and six pairs of oxen were required to drag it out of the city. Then he preached

*the Christian faith to the king and to all the people. And
through the miracle they had seen all believed perfectly in
Christ. The king had churches built in honor of God and in
reverence for the blessed knight San Giorgio. And when
everyone had been taught how to serve and to love God,
San Giorgio left the realm. Before leaving he gave to the
poor the noble horse that he had been riding and his knight's
armor, nobly and richly decorated, for the love of God.*

Arnaldo Fortini, *Francis of Assisi;*
A Translation of *Nova Vita di San Francesco*

• • • • • • • • • • • •

In the heart of a landlocked province of central Italy called
Umbria, the small town of Assisi cascades down the western
spur of Mount Subasio overlooking the alluvial plain of the
Spoleto valley. This region of Umbria is strewn with feudal
castles and fortified towers that dominate the region's rolling
peaks. It is adorned with cypresses and elms, mulberries, ox-
eye daisies and purple irises, and dense pine forests. Its lime-
stone crags and hills boast the deepest cave system in Italy.
Umbria's evening sunlight plays upon the land, lending olive
groves an odd luminescence and transforming evening skies
to fire and indigo. The region shines a magic that has seen a
disproportionate emergence of saints and not a few rogues.

During the unsettling period when Francis lived, violence
was engrained in the culture, and Assisi, as much as any
medieval Italian hill town, was swept into the tumult of the

age. By the time of Francis' birth in 1182 Assisi had been conquered by Rome, the Byzantine Empire, the Ostrogoths, the Lombards, and the Franks. A friar from the thirteenth century wrote: "We found in the ancient writings of Assisi, [that it] was surrounded by the strongest of walls and towers, adorned with palaces and strong structures, well populated with many gallant, high-spirited people, defended by numerous brave warriors, [and] was occupied by a terrible and ferocious people who inflicted havoc on all the surrounding land."[1]

Francis and Clare lived during the Middle Ages—the period of more or less a thousand years between the fall of the Roman Empire (fifth century) and the start of the Renaissance (sixteenth century). It was an era marked by brutal civil wars, assaults from barbarians, famine, misery, and priestly decay. The backdrop of the times was religious conflict, as the holy sites in Jerusalem had fallen to the Saracens (Muslims), and priests and merchants became crusading knights and warriors. Meanwhile, a corrupt Mother Church was vying for power with the Holy Roman Empire. The Church, having by this time held forth for a thousand years, still faced corruption in its own ranks, squalor among the masses, political wars, and the rise of alien beliefs. "When the thousand years are over, Satan will be released from his prison," says the book of Revelation. By the turn of the millennium in A.D. 1000—nearly two hundred years before Francis' time—pilgrims and priests were envisioning the coming of the end of the world.[2]

The Holy Roman Empire is considered to have been founded in about the tenth century by German princes who assumed the title "Emperor" through successive dynasties almost continuously up to the nineteenth century. Likening their role to that of the Caesars, these German princes therefore called their empire the "Roman" Empire, and heirs to the throne of this evolving power center were called "King of the Romans." The term "Holy" was added in the twelfth century.

In theory, in the early Middle Ages the emperor was to rule alongside the pope in a counterbalancing symbiosis: the pope was subject to the emperor politically, while the emperor bowed beneath the spiritual mantle of the pope, who crowned him. Around the turn of the millennium, as the world's end seemed to draw near, this mutuality manifested itself in secular emperors utilizing holy offices of the Church as tentacles of power.

Predictably, the mixing of religious office and political power eroded the congeniality. Relations disintegrated. In the late eleventh century an indignant Pope Gregory VII undertook sweeping reforms that prohibited further use of Church offices as imperial vassals. The pope and the then soon-to-be-emperor, King Henry IV of Germany, exchanged hostile attacks in letters that were a portent of the disintegration of relations that would define Church and empire throughout the Middle Ages.

Henry, still king—not yet emperor at the time[3]—issued the first volley in a scathing letter denouncing Pope Gregory's prohibitions and condemning him as a usurper to Saint Peter's throne (January 24, 1076):

[From] Henry, king not through usurpation but through the holy ordination of God, to Hildebrand [the pope's family name], at present not pope but false monk; you have shunned to rise up against the royal power conferred upon us by God, daring to threaten to divest us of it. As if we had received our kingdom from you! As if the kingdom and the empire were in your and not in God's hand! I, Henry, king by the grace of God, do say unto you, together with all our bishops: Descend, descend, to be damned throughout the ages.[4]

Pope Gregory responded in turn (February 22, 1076):

O Saint Peter, chief of the apostles, incline to us, I beg, your holy ears, and hear me. For the honor and security of your church, in the name of Almighty God, Father, Son and Holy Ghost, I withdraw, through your power and authority, from Henry the king, son of Henry the emperor, who has risen against your church with unheard of insolence, the rule over the whole kingdom of the Germans and over Italy. And I absolve all Christians from the bonds of the oath which they have made or shall make to him; and I forbid any one to serve him as king. I bind him in your stead with the chain of the anathema.[5]

In time, Pope Gregory revoked King Henry's ban, but the damage was irreversible. The controversy positioned the Church as an independent entity in political maneuverings, propelling what would become a prolonged struggle between popes and emperors for control of Europe. And as we shall see, some of the key figures in this struggle had close ties to Assisi.

Emperor Frederick I—Frederick "Barbarossa," who predated Francis by a generation—happened to live in a fortress above Assisi called La Rocca. In the aftermath of Gregory and Henry's antagonisms, Barbarossa saw it as his mission to assert the emperor's power over the ever-strengthening papacy. Among his many acts to this end, he added the term "holy" to the demarcation of the empire, forcefully asserting its "Holy Roman-ness." He also established (among other things) Roman laws and a legal constitution, which, given the chaos of the age, had been alien concepts. Moreover, because of Pope Gregory VII's decree forbidding bishops to be vassals of the state, Emperor Barbarossa established a network of dukes to maintain local order in their stead. But his attempt to impose the "rule of law" was not altogether embraced by his dukes, who preferred autonomous rule over their respective dominions. Barbarossa thus added yet another arm of power to consolidate his authority, the *ministerialia*—former military men. He hoped these men would prove serviceable and more loyal than the unruly dukes. This new order of armed champions became the defining model of military prowess of the age—noble knighthood.

And so the stage was set that would define the world of Francis and Clare.

• • • • • • • • • • • •

Assisi was well known as being feisty, of rushing riotously to arms at the first provocation. Like those of other fortress towns, citizens in Assisi celebrated weapons and carnage in a variety of city-sponsored festivities and religious festivals. A springtime celebration called Calendimaggio involved men from the upper part of town (the nobles) and those from the lower part (merchants) who would meet in the main piazza with blunted arms. After hurling insults and stones, a no-holds-barred melee broke out between the warring neighbors. Sometimes participants from surrounding towns joined in, elevating the games to outright battle. Young lads followed the lead of their older heroes to learn the art of combat. The games persisted until a dozen or more participants had been maimed or killed and one side finally conceded defeat. It was entertainment. Families could not exact revenge for the loss of life and limb.[6]

Ambition for war was also endemic in the culture, yet the power to orchestrate engagement lay with the overlords in the castles, the nobility. As Francis was growing up, however, a merchant class was rising and flourishing, and rumors abounded of uprisings in other localities. Assisi was strategically located along the primary route between Rome and France, the Strada Francesca. Tradesmen from Italy traveled this road endlessly, north to south, and Pietro

Bernadone, Francis' father, was numbered among the region's most prosperous; he regularly traveled to Champagne and Provence, where he bought and sold linens. Pietro and others returned home from France with colorful stories of wars and uprisings: working people in Picardy and Flanders were making war against the nobility. These actions were deemed treasonous acts of war by the emperor. And they were successful.

This marked the beginning of a trend that would sweep across the medieval landscape—the rise of the *comune* (commune), the portent of the demise of feudalism. The merchant class, or *mediani*, fueled the movement with aspirations of winning their share of the prize heretofore claimed exclusively by the nobility, the *maggiori*—that is, upward mobility. Their only means of asserting this claim was to make war. Furthermore, because of its association with knighthood, making war held out promise for the *mediani*—not only of achieving upward mobility but also of claiming rank by knighthood. Combat became a rite of passage and a test of moral grit. Aspirations for knighthood made war poetic.

About the time of Francis' birth, a coalition of the lower and merchant classes in Assisi had united to dismantle the system of government ruled by the nobles. They wanted a democratic arrangement that included governance by merchants, artisans, and workers of the field. Thus, the *mediani* challenged the *maggiori*, rebelling against heavy taxes and forced labor. In the second half of the twelfth century,

Italy experienced the decisive repulsion of imperial feudal entrenchment. Local towns waged self-contained class wars—Assisi's *sopra* (upper town) battled *il sotto* (lower town). At the same time, neighboring localities likewise waged wars between rival cities. Venice fought Genoa; Genoa fought Pisa; Pisa fought Lucca; Lodi fought Milan; Faenza fought Ravenna; Florence fought Siena; and Assisi fought Perugia. Francis and Clare would become improbable protagonists in their small town, which, as all small towns of the time, was inevitably drawn into the tumult of upheaval and revolution.

His mother was a Frenchwoman named Pica (from Picardy). Giving birth to her firstborn son while his father, Pietro, was on business in France, she named him Giovanni, after John the Baptist. But the boy's father returned and promptly rejected the religious association of the name in deference to one that held out a more promising destiny: he called him Francesco, "the French one." France was where Pietro had made his fortune. The name bestowed to the son all the dreams and optimism a father could bequeath to his firstborn. Pietro and Pica also had a second son, Francis' younger brother, Angelo.

The family home was nestled between two churches, the church of San Nicolo and the church of San Paolo, on the western tip of Assisi's main plaza, the Piazza del Comune. The piazza laid a line of demarcation between Assisi's landed nobility, who lived in the upper part of the town, and the rising merchant class, who dwelled on the lower end. The Bernadones lived in *il sotto*, while Clare's family, the noble Favorones of the house of Offreduccio, by contrast, lived in *la sopra* near the piazza of San Rufino. This was the exclusive section of town claimed by the nobility because of its proximity to the city's imperial fortress. Clare was born several years after Francis. So in the early years of Francis' youth, Clare would have been a toddler.

A town's main piazza was a festive place, boasting merchant fairs, public games, and jousts. Merchants who had traveled afar and who had returned with tales of extraordinary events would linger in the shops and the square telling their stories. This transformed the piazza into a gathering place and a conduit for the dissemination of local news, stories from faraway places, and exposure to differing cultures. Pietro Bernadone's shop faced Via Portica, a primary corridor for shoppers and merchants, while the family home faced the opposite direction opening to Via San Paolo. Since Via Portica and the Piazza del Comune were at the heartbeat of the din, the Bernadones were well positioned in the middle of town brawls, stories, and gossip.

Francis' childhood school was across town, toward the east, in a small church called San Giorgio. (Today the present-day Basilica of Santa Chiara subsumes it.) San Giorgio was a primary school for boys under the tutelage of the resident priest, and Francis would have attended between the ages of seven and ten (from about 1189 to 1192). This seems to have been the extent of his formal education. He learned Latin well enough to recite the

Lord's Prayer and say the Creed.[7] Otherwise, he is known to have used a bastardized mix of Latin and Umbrian (a precursor to Italian). He was an average student, and wrote poor Latin up to the day he died.

But he loved French, the native language of his mother. He spoke it often and sang it just as much, since as a young man he loved the French troubadours.[8] Troubadours traveled the countryside singing poems about brave knights and lady lovers. "He kisses her many times, saying, 'Oh sweet rose, what shall I do? For the light is coming and night is going away.'"[9] Francis likely learned these songs while traveling to France with his father on business. Around Assisi he became well known for singing the songs of the troubadours. Through these songs and stories, he became steeped in the grand tales of the champions they praised. The school he attended had in fact been named for one such hero, the legendary knight San Giorgio, whose devotion and valor in slaying the dragon was hailed throughout the Christianized world.[10]

The origins of the story of San Giorgio remain uncertain. He is thought to have been a British soldier named George who was put to death in April A.D. 303, under Diocletian. According to the fifth-century *Apocryphal Acts of Saint George*, he held the rank of tribune in the Roman army and was beheaded by Diocletian for protesting the emperor's persecution of Christians. George rapidly became venerated as an example of bravery and military prowess and thus was adopted as the patron saint of soldiers. In time it began to be reported during the Crusades that George appeared and aided the Christians in battle. Inevitably, George's reputation took on epic proportions and became the stuff of troubadour songs. His noble and courageous deeds, as noted by the poets, evolved to include his intervention on behalf of the helpless princess who had been destined to be sacrificed to a voracious dragon. The phantasmal elements of Saint George's story were first recorded in the late sixth century and seem to allude to the persecution of Diocletian, who in ancient texts was sometimes referred to as "the dragon." Some say the story became a Christianized version of the Greek legend of Perseus, who was said to have rescued the virgin Andromeda from a sea monster.[11]

Francis' childhood notions of heroism and devotion would have been shaped by this story. And not just this story, but also that of another hero who, like San Giorgio, lived in the third century and faced the hostility of the Roman Empire. He is Assisi's "other" saint, San Rufino, numbered among the many early converts to the unruly sect of people calling themselves Christians. Rufino had traveled throughout Italy converting many, until he settled in Assisi, where he became the town's first bishop. (There are no known records about the date of his coming.) By that time, however, he had provoked the hostility of the emperor, who demanded that his religious activities cease.[12] In support of the emperor, Assisi's proconsul ordered Rufino tortured with fire and threatened him with execution. Rufino is said to have responded, "I fear neither you nor your emperors!"[13] The proconsul thus ordered a millstone tied around his neck and had him thrown in the River Chiagio just west of Assisi. San Rufino was martyred sometime between 236 and 239.

The town's primary cathedral, which was dedicated to his memory, was completed in the mid-eleventh century, and Rufino became Assisi's patron saint. (Francis would eventually become the patron saint of Italy.) At the cathedral's dedication the people sang a battle song: *The martyr fights valiantly, like the lion; he does not know the meaning of defeat.*[14] Francis would have heard this song as a boy, and probably would have sung it many times. Assisi's patron saint Rufino conferred communal identity that rallied the devotion of the townspeople. He was their martyred hometown hero.

Other champions also fired the imagination of the impressionable young Francis. One was the archangel Michael, who, like Saint George, is said to have fought with a dragon and won, as noted in the book of the Apocalypse.[15] Michael's great battles with "his angels" brought him the stature of "commander of angels." After Francis' conversion, he accorded special devotion to Saint Michael the archangel, choosing his feast day (September 29) as one of the two times a year his order would convene. He regularly observed a forty-day fast that culminated on the feast day of Saint Michael.

But perhaps no heroic tale captured Francis' imagination as much as the tales of King Arthur and his Knights of the Round Table.[16] Francis' father's mobility would have enabled Pietro Bernadone to return with fabulous stories that he would hear during his travels to France, where Arthurian romance was flourishing. This is credited to the French writer Chrétien de Troyes, who wrote in the latter half of the twelfth century and is considered the inventor of Arthurian legend and courtly love.[17] No storyteller or -hearer could escape de Troyes' influence in southern France from the late twelfth and early thirteenth centuries.

Arthur's greatest knight was Sir Lancelot, who stood out among all the Knights of the Round Table as the bravest in combat, truest to duty, and most devoted in service to his king. He also serves, for de Troyes, as the culminating expression of chivalry in service to courtly love. In the tale titled "The Knight of the Cart," Queen Guinevere, Arthur's wife and Lancelot's lover, was taken captive in a distant land. She could gain her freedom only if a knight from Arthur's court won her freedom through battle. Arthur himself took up the challenge and went in pursuit of his queen, but Lancelot had gone before him. By the time Arthur caught up to Lancelot, it was clear to Arthur that the knight had already done battle along the way, as he was wounded and without his horse, yet fully dressed in armor. Still searching for Guinevere, and unaware of the king's presence behind him, the wounded and horseless Lancelot saw a cart approach. In those days carts were used to put criminals, traitors, murderers, and thieves on public display. Great shame was associated with riding in a cart. The saying arose: "Whenever you see a cart and cross its path, make the sign of the cross and remember God, so that evil will not befall you."[18]

King Arthur watched as Lancelot, laboring on foot, hurried after the cart and spoke to the dwarf who sat upon it. "Dwarf," he said, "in the name of God, tell me if you have seen my lady the queen pass by this way?"

The vile, low-born dwarf would give him no information; instead he said: "If you want to get into this cart I'm driving, by tomorrow you'll know what has become of the queen."

The dwarf immediately continued on his way, without slowing down even an instant for the knight, who hesitated but two steps before climbing in. . . .

Reason, who does not follow Love's command, told [the knight] to beware of getting in, and admonished and counseled him not to do anything for which he might incur disgrace or reproach. Reason, who dared tell him this, spoke from the lips, not from the heart; but Love, who held sway within his heart, urged and commanded him to climb into the cart at once. Because Love ordered and wished it, he jumped in; since Love ruled his action, the disgrace did not matter.[19]

Lancelot proceeded at great personal risk and exposure to save the queen. Reaching her ahead of Arthur, he battled her captors fiercely for her and won. The moment finally had come when he could claim his love. Seeing him, however, the queen turned her glance away and did not receive him.

Crushed in spirit, Lancelot assumed she had heard that he had jumped into a cart, bringing shame to his colors. He went to her a second time, and on this occasion she received him. He inquired if her rebuff had been due to his having ridden in a cart. The queen answered: "By delaying two steps you showed great unwillingness to climb into it. That, to tell the truth, is why I didn't wish to see you or speak with you."[20]

Courtly love, *amour courtois*, was idealized in the writings of Chrétien de Troyes and in the poetry of the twelfth-century French troubadours, who upheld love as all-subsuming devotion, overruling personal morality and even loyalty to the king. Lancelot was the queen's lover, and as a knight his heart "no longer belonged to him; rather it was promised to another, so he could not bestow it elsewhere. His heart was kept fixed on a single object by Love."[21]

Courtly love marked a revolution in attitudes about gender and sexuality. The lady was cherished as a poetic and personal inspiration, and no longer reduced to a disposable pawn in the manipulation of arranged marriages. The culture of knighthood, as glorified by the troubadour poets Francis emulated, elevated women as objects of love and duty whose favor was won only after the suitor (a knight) had courted her through vassalage—even if it meant personal and public shame.

So the themes of Francis' boyhood emerged. The fearless San Giorgio, the devoted San Rufino of Assisi, the faithful and romantic Lancelot—all manifested the ideals of medieval knighthood that shaped Francis' dreams and would fire his imagination to the end of his days.

CHAPTER
TWO

Partying and War

Besides a love for weapons, the age in which Francis lived also embodied a symbiotic celebration of pageantry, sensuality, and song. Those who knew Francis said of him that despite the banalities of the age, even at his worst he was likable and bighearted. But troubling points about his youth cannot be ignored. The earliest biographers wrote about these matters without reservation. As time went on, however, this part of his story evolved into obscurity and became excised from the official record. Inevitably, no one source captures a clear picture of Francis during these years before his life as a religious. And yet if one winnows through the various written narratives, noting points of consistency as well as points of incongruity, one finds that the sources, in concert, ultimately illuminate something of the *core* of the man Francis, both before and after his conversion.[1]

Early writers who addressed Francis' troublesome youth concur that he was popular and wild, loved parties and often funded them, and lived the life of a "playboy" (a term used in 2006 by Pope Benedict XVI to describe Francis' early life.[2]) The earliest biography about Francis was written in 1229 by Thomas of Celano, a follower and contemporary. Thomas writes that Francis' parents "reared him to arrogance in accordance with the vanity of the age. And by imitating their worthless life and character he himself was made more vain and arrogant."[3] He continues, "For a flawed tree grows from a flawed root. Then, without question, flowing on the tide of every kind of debauchery, they surrender themselves with all their energy to the service of outragious conduct." Centuries later, Arnaldo Fortini fills in the picture with details about the kinds of shameful practices in which the youth of Francis' time would have indulged. "To read in the contemporary chronicles the history of those days is to be astonished," Fortini writes. "We are transported at once to the strange eccentric, paradoxical Middle Ages, a time full of contradictions, furies, and bizarre practices. Lewd priests, libertine men, and half-dressed women joined the rowdy youths."[4]

The group of "rowdy youths" assigned one of their peers as *dominus* (king), to whom would fall the duties of arranging the banquet and footing the bill. Francis often received the scepter and freely answered this call, hosting the parties in a large hall or courtyard adorned with tapestries, flowers, and alluring women. At the end of the supper the company would parade through the streets of Assisi, singing love songs and waking neighbors. Francis surpassed them all in a "strong, sweet, clear and sonorous voice," notes his biographer Thomas of Celano, adding, "This is the wretched early training in which that man whom we today venerate as a saint passed his time from childhood and miserably wasted and squandered his time almost up to the twenty-fifth year of his life." Francis "was given over to revelry and song with his friends, roaming day and night throughout the city of Assisi. He was the most lavish in spending, so much so that all he could possess and earn was squandered on feasting and other pursuits, in songs, in soft and flowering garments, for he was very rich."[5]

Francis was known to be a smallish man, barely five foot three, with delicate features and large shining eyes. He sat well on his horse, his small stature aside, and deftly commanded his father's turf as chief trendsetter in all styles French. He wore satin and velvet and ran all over town commending his wares with a bow to the ladies or a lift of his cap to crusty old men. Were it anyone else, they might be provoked by such charms. But the young Francis, with his generous smile and his love songs in French, fired the affections of onlooking neighbors and stole the hearts of the ladies in town. His money sack was ever draining, spent on wine for the parties and tossing fistfuls to the poor. His parents replenished it constantly, and none blamed them.

Even the neighbors beyond his class, the nobility on the other side of town, knew the name of the son of Pietro Bernadone. Clare, a child at the time, who was blossoming into a town beauty, would have heard of his songs and his charms with the ladies. She herself stayed home, too rich and demure to join in the merriment. But the name of Francis was discussed in that home, as it was in many homes, and the time was approaching when it would be linked to her own.

Later versions of Francis' life gloss over or eliminate references to this extravagant misspent youth. Thomas of Celano's second biography of Francis titled *Remembrances* and also called the *Second Life* (written in 1247),[6] contrasts starkly to his earlier account. Describing Francis' youth, he now says, "He completely rejected anything that could sound insulting to anyone. No one felt a young man of such noble manners could be born of the stock of those who were called his parents."[7] Bonaventure, in his *Major Life* (1263), writes, "While living among humans, he was an imitator of angelic purity."[8] In any case, historians concur that even at his worst, Francis was not boorish nor prurient nor cruel. He was kind and happy, fully relishing the merrymaking of Assisi's younger crowd and accepting the scepter as "king of the party."

• • • • • • • • • • • •

During Francis' youth, a critical event occurred that similarly would have played heavily in shaping him. Assisi's revolt of 1198 became a defining episode for the town and, by implication, for Francis. It was his first opportunity to lay claim to the dreams of aspiring knighthood, and this in service to the greater cause of the social and economic advancement of the merchant class, his fellow *mediani*.

In that same year Pope Innocent III came to power. Innocent, then young and untested,[9] was facing threats against papal authority as the country became overruled by the growing force of the Holy Roman Empire. Upon his ascendancy, the new pope undertook immediately to consolidate central Italy and reclaim it under papal rule. Innocent went from region to region in the effort to win the promise from local dukes to abandon allegiance to the empire and cast their lot with the Church (becoming "papal" rather than "imperial").

The imperial representative at Spoleto, which governed Assisi and neighboring towns, was a duke named Conrad. In fact, Conrad sometimes lived in the imperial fort in Assisi, Barbarossa's former dwelling called La Rocca. Conrad responded to Innocent III's entreaties by surrendering his dominion to papal control, abdicating allegiance to Holy Rome. Nevertheless, neither Conrad, the pope, the emperor, nor any other duke had anticipated that the people of Assisi had plans of their own. And those plans did not include popes or dukes.

In the aftermath of Conrad's decision, Assisi's *mediani* incited open rebellion against the *maggiore*, raising their swords against both the Church and the empire in the name of the commune. Assisi's merchant class wanted independence, and Assisi was ready to wage war on itself to claim it. It began when Conrad left his residency in La Rocca to undertake the necessary legalities involved with the change of allegiance. While he was away, Assisi's merchant-class warriors, sixteen-year-old Francis among them, laid siege to the fortress.[10] They pulled stone after stone from the fort's white rugged walls until the whole fortress was dismantled and razed.[11] Thus began a civil war in Assisi that soon extended well beyond the destruction of the fortress, spilling onto the city streets. The *mediani* routed castles and other strongholds of feudalism, driving noble families from their homes. Nobles who had known only affluence and prestige were left without roofs over their heads. Many of them fled Assisi for its hated rival city, Perugia, due west. Clare's family and Clare herself were among those driven from their homes. It is therefore remotely possible that Francis' first direct encounter with Clare was in the context of war, terrorizing her and her family and routing them from town. Historical documents record that many feudal families fled and never returned during this violent period in Assisi's history.[12]

The civil war lasted for the next few years. Assisi's merchant-class warriors ambushed nearby castles and feudal lords, who retaliated with ferocity. As a defensive measure, Assisi's citizens erected—in an incredibly short period of time—towers and the wall around their city. Some assert that Francis' experience in dismantling the fortress and castles and then building the city wall made him the expert stonemason he later demonstrated as a religious, when he would use that skill to rebuild ruined churches.

For the next two years, from 1198 to 1200, Assisi and Perugia existed in a state of guerrilla warfare that included raids, ambushes, border skirmishes, and reprisals. In October 1201 Perugia sought a pact with the nearby town of Foligno "for the safety of the city of Perugia and of the men who live in it."[13] Assisi received aid from neighboring Nocera, Bevagna, Spello, Rosciano, Fabriano, and surrounding *castelli* (castles).

In November 1202 the displaced noble lords from Assisi who had been exiled to Perugia decided along with the Perugini themselves to take back their city, and they declared war against Assisi. Always ready for a fight, Assisi answered the challenge. On a brisk November morning, the city's warring contingent left the city gate led by a chariot bearing the colors of the commune, blue and red, with the crest of a lion and a cross. Francis was numbered among the *Campagnia dei Cavalieri*—the city's elite corps of armed companies made up of knights and prosperous merchants who could afford a horse and armor. As the bells of the commune announced the soldiers' advance, he marched side by side with shoe smiths, butchers, clothiers turned archers, riders, and knights. The small but imposing band of local warriors wended their way down the road through the plain until they came to the midway point between Perugia and Assisi, a hill called Collestrada. There they were to meet the enemy.

As evening fell, all sides savored a moment of peace before the ensuing battle. Throughout both camps would have echoed the sounds of chain mail tumbling to the ground, and helmets, swords, rapiers, lances, and shields being lain down in temporary rest. As evening settled into night, Assisi's warriors anticipated the glory they would win for their town. Some would have tied a relic thread from the robe of San Rufino to the hilt of their sword for protection in battle.

When dawn broke, Assisi's men, Francis among them, armed themselves and mounted their horses. (To be "armed" in the Middle Ages meant to put on armor.) In short order, knights charged, lances aimed straight, and the Assisiani advanced to take the first knoll—a victory that rallied them. Each side fought with equal fury as the battle moved over the hill of Collestrada into surrounding woodlands. But the tide quickly changed for Assisi. A chronicler of the time described the routing of Assisi's army: *strages latissima, cedes severissima*—"the final defeat came late, but the slaughter was very severe."[14] Hunted, hacked, and dismembered, the troops were crushed on the plain near the bridge at Collestrada. The blood of Francis' friends and compatriots turned the waters of the Tiber River rank. A thirteenth-century poet recounts the grim scene:

How could the Assisiani pretend to be ignorant of your strength? Oh, how disfigured are the bodies on the field of battle, and how mutilated and broken are their members. The hand is not to be found with the

foot, nor the entrails joined to the chest; on the fore-
head horrible windows open out instead of eyes. That
no prophet, interrogated before the battle, could have
seen such omens! Oh, you of Assisi, what a sad day
and what a dark hour was this!

The poet concludes: *cecidere potentes Assisii*—"Mighty
Assisi was beaten."[15]

We do not know how many men Francis maimed or
killed in battle that day. The fact that he survived so savage
a slaughter implies that he fought with courage and ferocity. But the Perugini, recognizing class differences between
foot and horse soldiers, knew the advantage of taking riders
as prisoners for ransom, and Francis' armor signaled wealth
in the family. The enemy reckoned it expedient to take him
hostage. So in the devastating aftermath of the battle at
Collestrada, Francis, the son of Pietro Bernadone, was
taken a prisoner of war.

THREE

Dreams and Prayers

Among Francis' fellow prisoners in Perugia was a knight from Apulia, in the south, who had come north to fight with the Assisiani.[1] He was awash with stories about Gautier de Brienne, a French knight of high birth from a military family, who had undertaken a military campaign in the south. Stories of the famous Gautier's daring military successes abounded throughout France and Italy.

Francis' fellow prisoner recounted a battle under Gautier's leadership that had taken place in June 1201 in Capua. With only a few hundred French knights in a single-line phalanx, Gautier had assaulted an imperial army of five thousand. The French knights fought with ferocity, and the Germans were soundly defeated. The victory was considered a miracle, and

Gautier's reputation as a warrior of spirit, honor, and courage had been burnished to epic proportions.[2] In the dark, damp underground prison, with no light, latrine, or heat, and little nourishment, Francis suffered fevers and at times delirium. Yet hearing about Gautier aroused longings in him. He wanted to follow the brave knight and fight with him, of whom it was said he had never known shame or defeat.

In the meantime, Assisi and Perugia were still at odds with each other, and Assisi was at odds with itself as well. In June 1203 Assisi's *maggiore*, who had fought on the side of Perugia at Collestrada, wanted to return to their homes. But unresolved tension remained. How could fellow citizens of such a small town live in peace among the very neighbors who had destroyed their homes and livelihood? All sides understood that if Assisi was to survive and thrive as a rising commune, there must be a degree of reconciliation, so they named arbiters to draw up a document—a Peace Paper: "Because there is in Assisi discord between the [nobility] and the men of the people over the destruction of the castles and feudal servitude."[3] The peace agreement listed the names of feudal lords whose homes had been destroyed, ordered that the commune construct new houses and towers, and outlined the dimensions of the buildings to be erected and the districts that were to be rebuilt.[4]

Nearly a year passed with Francis languishing in prison. Finally, as part of the peace accord with Assisi, the Perugini made possible the release of their sickest captives. Francis, whose father was permitted to buy his freedom, was among them. But the squalid conditions of his captivity and intimate contact with fellow prisoners had exposed him to the rampant contagions of the time, including malaria and tuberculosis. He was gravely ill. After having spent a year of living in squalor and exposure of the prison dungeon, Francis would spend another year at home recovering.

The next two years began a prolonged heartbreaking period for Francis that is shrouded in mystery. However, there is general agreement on a few points. The first is that his experience with war, prison, and illness had a tempering effect on him. The second is that over the next few years this tempering ultimately led to his renunciation of family, his conversion to a literal appropriation of the teachings of Jesus as denoted in the Gospel, and allegiance to a life of poverty.

Upon his return to Assisi, probably late in 1203, the once effervescent and ebullient son of Pietro Bernadone was pale, emaciated, and walked with a stick. The piazza near his home was, as always, filled with peddlers and merchants and activity that had once served as Francis' stage. But his days of running up and down Assisi's alleys singing troubadour songs, making war, and chasing women were gone. It was all he could do to climb the pink-stone stairway in his home.

In early 1204, after a year of recovery from his prison time, Francis was beginning to feel inner changes. He was unsettled, agitated, sometimes depressed, and other times wildly animated. Something was stirring inside him. Many historians mark this period as the beginning of Francis' spiritual calling. But such things are difficult to document. In any case, his health slowly improved and he resumed a degree of normalcy in his life, returning to his father's shop to work. He also turned again to the partying habits of the local youth.

During this time two possibilities emerged that reinvigorated him and harkened the animated Francis that had always endeared people so. The first was a summons by the great French knight Gautier de Brienne: he was soliciting the swords and devotion of knights for a campaign he had undertaken in Apulia in southern Italy. Gautier's aim was to reclaim the region for the Normans, whose reign had been usurped by German overlords. A young noble living in Assisi told Francis about his intention to join Gautier, and thus rekindled Francis' aspirations for knighthood.[5] According to Thomas of Celano, Francis had a dream one night that spurred his desire. "In the sweetness of grace it seemed to him that his whole house was filled with soldiers' arms: saddles, shields, spears and other equipment."[6] Francis arose the next morning "with a happy spirit. Considering his vision a prediction of great success, he felt sure that his upcoming journey to Apulia would be successful."[7] Francis was determined not to miss another chance at achieving his long-awaited dream of knighthood. He would transform the brutalities and miseries of Collestrada and turn his shame into valor. He would make a mockery of the mockers who had denounced the defeated Assisiani as cowards. He would advance the cause of justice, fighting with the great Gautier de Brienne and claiming allegiance alongside his elite warriors, who scaled walls and conquered castles and never tasted defeat. He would kneel before the altar and be consecrated by Gautier a courageous and faithful knight—in the name of God, in the name of Saint George, and in the name of Saint Michael. Francis would answer the call: "My soul to God, my life to the king, my heart to my lady." Thus, awakening, Francis "got up with great joy [and] thought in a worldly way that he must be singled out magnificently, and he considered the vision a portent of future good fortune. He resolved to undertake the journey to Apulia to be knighted."[8]

It was late 1204 when Francis met at Assisi's piazza of San Rufino with nine other warriors and yeomen, all bound for Spoleto. There, all regional militia were to gather and travel together to join Gautier's forces in Apulia. Before the troops set out, the bishop blessed them and made the sign of the cross over them. The departure of knights for battle was a community event and a spectacle of color and solemnity. The town would have turned out for their leave-taking to hear the blessing of the bishop and to wish Godspeed to their neighbors, husbands, friends, and lovers who now took up arms. The warriors gathered near the cathedral of San Rufino. Clare's family home overlooked the piazza, so she would have witnessed the grand event and recognized the well-known Francis Bernadone as numbered among the mounted. Then, leaving Assisi, Francis rode high on his horse alongside the noble comrade in arms who had encouraged him to join. His spirit was so elevated that people asked him the reason for his delight. He answered, "I know that I shall become a great prince!" Then he passed out of the city gate carried on the dream of a royal homecoming.[9]

The story ends badly. Francis and his traveling companion made it to Spoleto, fifteen miles south of Assisi. But there Francis' malarial fever returned. He spent the night shivering and sweating, in and out of delirium, and saw another vision. This one said, "Go home."[10] He returned to Assisi a few days later, not as a prince but as a failure.

Gautier's campaign in the south also took a bad turn. Shortly after Francis returned home, his hero Gautier was fighting near Naples when he was taken by a surprise attack. He and his company were routed. Gautier fought heroically but was felled by wounds from a shower of arrows. He was taken to the German overlord whose forces had conquered him and who, seeing great profit in owning the living legend, promptly set about trying to save him. Gautier began to recover, and for a time it looked as if he might survive. At this point his German captor proposed to the knight that he change sides and become his ally. Gautier, being loyal and noble, refused. Enraged, the German lord insulted the great knight and threatened him with torture. Gautier refused to render such power to his enemy; he took off his bandages and allowed his wounds to worsen to the point of death. He died in June 1205.[11]

• • • • • • • • • • • •

Francis sought solace after his failure by again embracing the frivolities of his former way of life. As in the old days, his carousing friends crowned him their *dominus* and handed him the kingly scepter. "A few days after he returned to Assisi, one evening his friends chose him to be in charge so that, according to his whim, he would pay their expenses. He made arrangements for a sumptuous banquet, as he had done so often in the past." Yet, while the friends were hooting and singing, Francis tarried behind. He seemed "a lonely boy," as one friar described it. "When they left the house bloated, his friends walked ahead of him, singing throughout the city. Holding in his hand the scepter of his office, he fell slightly behind them. He was not singing, but was deeply preoccupied." His companions were nonplussed and jibed him. "'What were you thinking about that you did not follow us? Were you perhaps thinking about taking a wife?'"[12]

This introduces the second possibility that emerged for Francis at this time and brought him back to life. There was talk among his friends of a girlfriend—and Francis conceded that indeed he did have a girlfriend. Multiple sources concur that he answered: "You are right! I was thinking about taking a wife more noble, wealthier, and more beautiful than you have ever seen."[13] And "'I will take a bride more noble and more beautiful than you have ever seen, and she will surpass the rest in beauty and excel all others in wisdom.'"[14]

Much ink has been spilled debating whether this noble and beautiful bride Francis dreamed about was "true religion," as interpreted by Thomas of Celano, or "Lady poverty," as suggested by another early writer in a document called *The Legend of the Three Companions* (Bonaventure makes no mention of the incident).[15] The obscurity surrounding this period of Francis' life of course raises questions. Since he had been raised in and had fully embraced the aptitude of the burgeoning merchant class; since he had lived his youth driven by the flesh in all of its manifestations; and since coming of age he had aimed solely for the worldly glory of knighthood, how did he become interested in religion? A leading friar at the Sacro Convento put it another way: "What was the internal energy that changed Francis?" It is a reasonable question.

It is clear that during the years 1204 and 1205, in which there was talk of a girlfriend, there was also evidence of an emerging interest in religion. Francis—now age twenty-two or twenty-three—was retreating regularly to caves in the crannies of Mount Subasio to spend time praying. Accompanied and supported by an intimate, helpful, and unnamed friend, Francis regularly went "to remote places, suitable for talking, asserting that he had found a great and valuable treasure." Thomas of Celano notes that Francis loved this secret friend "more than all the rest" because of the "constant intimacy of their mutual love" between the two, and that he shared with this friend the secrets of his inner turmoil. The friend stood by him throughout the two subsequent years of inner battles, flesh against spirit.[16] His friend "gladly went with him whenever he was summoned" by Francis, and they often secretly went to a special cave in Mount Subasio to talk about "the treasure."[17] Francis "spoke to him mysteriously, but did not reveal his secret purpose entirely. Moreover, flooded with a new spirit, Francis frequently entered a certain cave, while his companion waited outside."[18] Also, according to Thomas, these episodes at the caves included an element of temptation: "As he began to visit hidden places conducive to prayer, the devil struggled to drive him away with an evil trick." He perceived God speaking to him in response: "Francis, you have traded what you loved in a fleshly empty way for things of the spirit, *taking the bitter for the sweet*. When the order is reversed, the things I say will taste sweet to you even though they seem the opposite."[19]

The dissonance and obscurity behind the girlfriend question and the praying in caves as they relate to Francis' prolonged conversion raise more questions than they resolve. If he had fallen in love with religion or poverty, as some writers assert, why would he have waited two more years before claiming it in a public and decisive way? (Biographers locate Francis' conversion as having occurred twenty years before his death, which occurred in 1226. This locates the year of his conversion as 1206, two years after the praying in caves and the talk of a girlfriend.) We have already seen that whenever Francis felt anything strongly, he acted upon it decisively, immediately, concretely, and sometimes outrageously. When he had the dream about the arms, he polished his mail. When he severed his bond with his family—as will be discussed—he not only said good-bye but also stripped off the family clothes and stood naked before the assembly. When he was to receive a "vision" from God telling him to "rebuild my church," he picked up stones. He did not live in abstractions.

Francis himself answers the question. In his *Testament*, which was dictated in the weeks preceding his death in 1226, he says, "The Lord gave me, Brother Francis, thus to begin doing penance in this way: for when I was still in sin, it seemed too bitter for me to see lepers. And the Lord Himself led me among them and *I showed mercy* to them. And when I left them, what had seemed bitter to me was turned into sweetness of soul and body. And afterwards I delayed a little and left the world."[20] He intended his *Testament* to be a final word of exhortation and encouragement to his languishing companions and to the order. His words carry the authority of approaching death. He meant them to be authoritative. Brother Leo, Francis' scribe, would have written them with utmost care, and the brothers would have preserved them with vigilance. Therefore, what he says in his *Testament* ought to be taken at face value and understood to be the truth as Francis himself understood it.

Before the episode with the lepers, which biographers concur took place in 1206, Francis, by his own testimony, was "still in [his] sins." Before "leaving the world" he was well known in Assisi as being brave, high-spirited, popular, kind, poetic, and romantic. But Francis' inner life was moving him in a different direction. During these obscure years, he was praying in caves, and his deliberations involved evil suggestion. At the same time, Francis was pulling back from his partying friends who perceived (rightly) that he was falling in love. Whereas his testimony does not answer what temptation was seizing him at the time, the notion may have involved the girlfriend. If the girlfriend was merely a metaphor for his love of religion or poverty, then it contradicts what he said in his last testament. This leaves the love question unresolved. In the meantime, he spent a great deal of time in caves with an unidentified friend who was helping Francis by waiting outside the caves while Francis wrestled inside himself with temptation of a carnal nature.

If womanizing and carousing were no longer driving him, what temptation seized him in the throes of these inner battles in the caves?[21] What if, despite emerging religious inclinations, Francis was feeling tempted by love for the girlfriend? What if, as he himself answered when asked about it, she had indeed been rich and noble and beautiful and wise?

Light Breaks

This brings us to Clare.

Friars, scholars, historians, scientists, tour guides, nuns, and theologians find plenty to argue about regarding Francis and Clare's mysterious bond. There is, however, general agreement on two points. First, Clare of Assisi was irrefutably a primary force in Francis' life. To know Francis truly one must also know Clare. Sister Chiara Anastasia, a nun of the Order of the Poor Clares who currently lives cloistered in Assisi, said of Clare's love for Francis, "After God, he is the person who helped her most in her spiritual journey. She uses strong expressions to express how important he was to her. Francis was a mediator in her life." Brother Loek Bosch, a friar (Observant) who lives at San Damiano, says, "You cannot dream of Clare without Francis, and you cannot dream of Francis without Clare." Angela Maria Seracchioli, author and expert on medieval pilgrimage, says, "Francis could doubt everybody but Clare. Clare was the woman married to Francis in the soul, [citing author Peiro Bargellini] 'on whom the fatigue of the man can rest.'"

Second, whatever their relationship had been before their respective conversions, after their religious vows it remained pure. But the agreement ends there. No topic relating to Francis evokes more winces, rolling eyes, pregnant pauses, darting glances, and general agitation than does the question of Clare's relationship to him and how it manifested itself.

Some say the social barriers that separated them would have precluded their having met before their religious lives. Others concede that because Assisi was a small town, and because of the extraordinary stature of both personalities— Clare's well-attested beauty and Francis' well-known popularity among women—it is inevitable that they would have come to know each other.

The official Catholic position asserts that their bond, while extraordinary, can be likened to that of a father and daughter. For this they cite the alleged age difference: it is widely agreed that Francis was born in 1182 (some say 1181); Clare's birth date is unknown. It is thought to be in or around 1192 to 1194, but even these dates are not verifiable. Except for the year of her canonization in 1255, little to nothing exists in the official archival record about Clare. Ultimately the age difference is irrelevant. During the Middle Ages young women of the nobility, as early as thirteen or fourteen, were being groomed for marriages of rank, frequently to men who were much older. Clare was not exempt. Witnesses in the canonization investigation attested that as a teenager she was being prepared for marriage.

Civic archives do leave a clear record about the nobility of Clare's lineage, however. Her paternal great-great-grandfather was a nobleman named Offredo. Her great-grandfather was Bernardino. Her grandfather thus was called Offreduccio di Bernardino, a powerful count. Offreduccio had at least three sons: Scipione di Offreduccio, Monaldo, and Favorone, Clare's father. "They were all strong, daring, cruel, known for their bravura in the use of the spear and the halberd."[1] Clare's father was a knight and known to ride into battle with a drawn sword. The family descended from the Lombards and Franks and was connected to and supportive of Frederick of Barbarossa and distantly related to the popes of the period.[2] Clare's mother, Ortolana, also of noble lineage, was linked to the same German line from which arose Frederick II. Clare had two sisters: Catherine (later called Agnes) and Beatrice.

The absence of concrete historical data regarding Clare herself has left researchers understandably frustrated. Some points, however, can be gleaned from early documents related to Clare, specifically hagiographies and the remembrances of those who testified as sworn witnesses after Clare's death during the canonization investigation.[3] From these writings a composite picture of Clare can be sketched that fills in otherwise obscure details about her role in Francis' life during the years of his religious awakening and following. (The time period during which Francis and Clare's relationship comes into clearer focus in the sources begins broadly around the year 1206.)

One (male) witness in the canonization investigation, a citizen of Assisi—one Lord Ranieri di Bernardo—recounts that Clare was strikingly beautiful. The same witness attests that her parents were grooming her for marriage in her early teen years and that she was being solicited by many suitors of high rank, Ranieri among them. He said as well that Clare rebuffed them all. He and others attest that during her teen years Clare was one of Assisi's most sought-after noble maidens. Even so, sisters in the cloister who remembered Clare as a young girl testified that she was quiet and demure and remained in the family home more so than in the city square. Despite her nobility, she was bighearted toward the poor. More than one witness mentioned how she often took food from the family table to set aside for beggars.

Others who were intimately acquainted with Clare's home life (her blood sister, for one, and the house watchman, for another) recounted that during the years before she joined Francis, she had adopted the habits of a penitent. Under the silk gowns and delicate linens that marked the refinement of the nobility, she put on an abrasive, coarse hair shirt, the mark of the penitent. (It was intended to keep Christ's discomfort ever in mind and to elevate one's dependency on God.) Clare is also known to have prayed frequently, counting her prayers in piles of pebbles, and she began to fast regularly. Her blood sister Beatrice described how Clare sold all of her own inheritance and part of Beatrice's to give the money to the poor. The sources attest that during this period, when Francis aimed to rebuild ruined churches in the early stage of his life as a religious, Clare gave him money toward the repair of one church, the Portiuncula, which later became the seat of his order.

The sources also make it clear that though Francis had no intention of starting a "movement" from the outset, as he proceeded to rebuild ruined churches after his conversion, he intended for one of the sites (San Damiano) to house women.[4] The implication is that Francis and Clare knew each other during the years when he was moving toward religious conversion—since during this time he resolved to rebuild the church. In any case, it is attested by witnesses that in the years associated with his conversion, Clare and Francis were meeting clandestinely.[5] "He visited her and she more frequently him, moderating the times of their visits so that this divine pursuit could not be perceived by anyone nor objected to by gossip."[6]

Therefore, it is impossible to understand the life of Francis without confronting this relationship and the force it wielded in Francis' renunciation of class and rank to take the garb of a penitent, and Clare's subsequent decision to do the same.

* * * * * * * * * * * * *

In late 1205, when Francis was retreating to caves, his hero Gautier de Brienne was dead, and so were Francis' dreams of knighthood. He was unresolved, wrestling with himself, agitated by love of some sort. The inner turmoil he was experiencing would culminate in religious vows, but his religious life did not come to him as an epiphany. It involved a prolonged, gradual, sometimes tortured process that carried the effects of a multiplicity of forces.

The retreats to the caves settled him. He began to perceive the power of the land and to sense vitality in the silence of living things. He opened to the beauty of the forest. The holm oaks and cypresses, the bluebells, foxgloves, and ferns all reached upward for light from beneath the shadows, quiet movements of creation that felt to him enduring and hopeful. He listened to birds. He grew to love the skylark, "a humble bird [that] walks contentedly along the road to find grain, even if she finds it among rubbish."[7] (The lark's earth-colored mantle would become the signature color of Francis' tunic.) He began to understand the mystery of physical creation as the reflection of spiritual re-creation.

Also during this time he came under the influence of a grassroots movement called *Ordo Poenitentium*, "the penitential order." During the Middle Ages in the West, religious options (so to speak) were limited. If one was not a Catholic, one was outside God's graces. Yet the well-known corruptions of the Church proved problematic for some earnest seekers. The penitential movement provided an alternative for those stouthearted religious souls who claimed loyalty to the Church but eschewed its trappings.

The *Ordo Poenitentium* reform movement is credited for the proliferation of monasteries and hermitages that gained wide popularity among laity, clergy, oblates, hermits, and pilgrims—especially in the centuries preceding Francis' conversion. It showed itself through poverty, mendicant preaching, and acts of mercy toward outcasts and lepers. Early on, as the movement gained momentum, the Mother Church contended with other distractions that for a time left these expressions of religious enthusiasm without direction and oversight. Inevitably this contributed to the flowering of heresies, which in time compelled Church authorities to take note. As a result, when Francis was moving in this direction, the Church was skeptical about rendering legitimacy to the multiplicity of penitential bands arising on the scene. Francis would be instrumental in overcoming this reticence.

At this early stage, however, as Francis worked through his inner questioning, he came to recognize that the only honest choice for him in pursuit of a religious life was to embrace a vow of penitence. Francis could do nothing halfway.

Sensing the possibility of spiritual re-creation as metaphorically expressed in the design of creation, and resonating with the simplicity and gratitude that marked the penitents, by early 1206 Francis decided to make a pilgrimage. All over Europe, pilgrim roads stretched north to south leading to holy sites in Rome, Jerusalem, and Spain. Francis wanted to visit the holy relics of beloved saints Peter and Paul in Rome. That was common practice in the Middle Ages—tens of thousands of pilgrims could visit those shrines in a single day.

Some travelers went for healing, others for penance. The trek itself purified the penitent—hunger, bracing winds, rain, illness, and the threat of bandits all tested their resolve and prepared them for miracles they were sure would meet them. Pilgrims traveled in bands and stayed in monasteries and hospices along the standard routes. They used their cloaks as a blanket and their staffs as a walking tool—or a weapon of defense, should the need arise. One hospice was rarely more than a day's travel from the next, and the pilgrims tried to travel before dark, when bandits emerged. Their hosts might provide them a new set of shoes or a coin in exchange for prayers before the relics. Unlike his departure for Apulia—when he was mounted, armed, and bearing the colors of his town—Francis left for Rome in a pilgrim's cloak and cap, and carried only a staff and a sack with hard bread and wine. This time, passing through Assisi's city gate with fellow penitents, he made no claims about becoming a prince.

In Rome Francis and his company would have converged in the piazza, singing and chanting in front of the basilica of Saint Peter. Pilgrims carrying oil lamps would have entered through vaulted archways until they reached the holy tomb. They would have knelt and touched their foreheads to the altar. Some pilgrims would have tossed coins through the small window of the burial chamber.[8]

This being a church, beggars amassed. Maimed or crippled, blind or paralyzed, they wept and muttered and waved bony hands, tapping sticks and asking for alms. Francis had always been uncomfortable around such people. Yet now, in Rome, he inexplicably exchanged his pilgrim clothes for the disheveled garb of the wretches, entering with them to the atrium, where deacons of the Church served food to the poor. Perhaps in spite of himself he felt a resonance in their midst. He would say later that were it not for his fear of being scorned by his fellow travelers, he would have returned to the beggars and assumed their garb again and again.[9]

Yet he did fear his fellow travelers' scorn. The idea of embracing a life of poverty had not yet consumed him. So he returned to his pilgrim's clothes and joined his townsmen for the journey back home.

●●●●●●●●●●●●●

It is still 1206, and Francis has not abandoned the clothes of a merchant's son. "The man of God, Francis," Bonaventure says, "did all these things while not yet withdrawn from the world in attire and way of life."[10] For all his good feelings amid the poor in Rome, Francis was absolutely repulsed by lepers. His revulsion typified the general social attitudes of the time. Lepers, rich or poor, were cared for by the commune in leper hospitals, foul and fetid places to which no normal human being would willingly submit. Neither did many of the infected persons. In that case, they would be snitched upon by fearful neighbors, friends, and sometimes even family members. The leper would then be forcibly removed from his or her home and forever banished from day-to-day life. Many leper hospitals existed in and around Assisi. During his comings and goings on his father's business, Francis did all he could to avoid them. Pietro Bernadone owned land in the valley, so inevitably Francis would sometimes be compelled to pass by them. Whenever he did, he covered his nose.

One day Francis had gone south of town to settle accounts on land owned by his father. Upon his return, as he sat on his horse, the sound of a leper waving his rattle on a stick (required by law as a warning to others) stopped him in his tracks. Francis had no fear of swords and war, but the stench of an approaching leper turned his heart cold.

So the moment arrived. This moment, of all moments that had scripted his unsettled life, rose as a storm behind his eyes. All that he had dreaded he might be and all that he feared he was becoming—all of it waved its rattle on that road that day. "God inspired me," Francis later said in his *Testament*. "The sight of lepers nauseated me beyond measure." The leper continued on his way, not slowing an instant. But Francis knew he must chase this ghost or forever be chased himself. He dismounted. He hesitated two steps. Then with the strength of youth and the speed of a horse, he ran to the leper and pulled the rotting flesh to his arms. Disgrace did not matter. Love ruled his actions. His fears met their death that day. The call of the rattle drove him to the place where he finally understood he could not outrun himself.

• • • • • • • • • • • •

Up to this point we have seen an earth-leaning Francis, a boy with dreams of San Giorgio; the *dominus* of Assisi's party crowd; a warrior and knight; a lover and troubadour poet. At the embrace of the leper, all sides of the man would change—one to the next, then to the next, and to the one after that, toppling one over the other. The entire makeup of the man turned inside out.

A friar posed the question, "What was the internal energy that changed him?" Put another way, what was the force that pulled him from his horse and drove him into the arms of a leper? This moment Francis concedes was the turning point of his life as a religious. Why was it the leper who galvanized this devotion? Again, the scientist says that to discern matter from antimatter one must measure the electric charge. The "electric charge" that proved the point of singularity for Francis—the bolt that triggered the transformation from Francis-the-Man to Francis-the-Religious—was the moment he embraced the leper. At that moment all allegiances went upside down, and there was no turning back. One biographer says he did violence to himself. Why violence? What kind of violence? Why the leper? Why flesh? Why *rotting* flesh?

Throughout his life Francis struggled with "grave temptation of the flesh," says Bonaventure. "In wintertime he would frequently immerse himself in a ditch filled with icy water and preserve the white robe of modesty from the flames of voluptuousness."[11] For his entire life he battled the desire to marry and have a family—even late in life, within a few years of his death:

> Once he opened the cell, went out into the garden and, throwing his poor still naked body into the deep snow, began to pack it together by the handful into seven mounds. Showing them to himself, he spoke as if to another person: "Here, the larger one is your wife; those four over there are your two sons and two daughters; the other two are a servant and a maid who are needed to serve them. Hurry, then, and get them some clothes because they are freezing to death! But if the complicated care of them is annoying, then take care to serve one Master!" A certain brother, who was *giving himself to prayer* at the time, saw *in the bright moonlight* all these things. When the man of God [Francis] learned that he had seen this that night, he ordered him to reveal to no living being what he had seen as long as he himself lived.[12]

Flesh—his flesh—proved the great antagonist to his aspirations as a religious. But becoming himself like a leper enabled Francis to crucify the last corner of his nature that couldn't be overcome by mere vows, dreams, tears, and prayers. He had one goal in mind: to conquer himself. Perhaps he thought if he made himself unclean there could be no more dreams of a wife and children. So he did violence to himself. "Doing violence to himself, he conquered himself."[13] Only an assault on the flesh could unbind the flesh. The leper cut down the part of his nature that he could not subdue. The leper was his baptism, his death—the final renunciation of the last vestige of desire he clung to. People thought Francis was mad, and he didn't argue the point. He hesitated two steps before his final gasping lurch toward the cart, to penance, the place of disgrace.

This inevitably begs the question, Could his dreams of a wife and family have had anything to do with Clare? During Clare's teen years, before she made her religious vows, she and Francis were meeting clandestinely. This may or may not suggest that Clare was the unnamed friend mentioned above who accompanied him during the season of his praying in the caves. (In any case, it shows they were not averse to the idea of secret meetings.) It does, however, clearly indicate that his choice to embrace a life of poverty influenced her decisions not to marry and to posture herself for the same destiny.

When Francis was praying in the caves, he wrestled (as mentioned by Thomas of Celano) with a temptation of the flesh. There was also talk among his friends during this time of a girlfriend, which he confirmed. All the while, he was feeling movements of heart that inclined him toward religion. Clare, too, was experiencing spiritual pining, as noted by those who knew her at home. He was advancing in his spiritual vision while she, under his guidance, was advancing in hers. The religious mood of the times would destine them to embrace the *Ordo Poenitentium*, the equivalent to a grassroots religious movement that did not demand the priestly track. But it did demand certain renunciations, including carnal ones. The flesh was the final enemy for Francis. He felled it by the embrace of the leper.

As the story unfolds, it seems apparent that Francis and Clare broke rank together. Out of an increasing love for God and (this writer asserts) in the throes of an unresolved mutual love for each other (both at once and both thoroughly), he acted first and prepared the way for Clare to follow, which, as will be seen, she did a few years later.

The turning point took place on the road at the dismount. After the race to the arms of the leper, *Franciscum scilicet omnen*—"Francis changed utterly."[14]

Endings

The transaction with the leper toppled all outworkings of his pre-conversion life. And as we shall soon see, it carried similar effects for Clare.

Francis says in his *Testament,* "I tarried yet a little while," then left the world. This "tarrying" demands further elucidation, for it traces the final decisive break that would definitively transform Assisi's well-known, well-loved troubadour into someone the townspeople were not sure they recognized. Here, though, the record is inconsistent, so we are left to cobble together the main features of the events that transpired over the next few months.

The time is late 1206 and Francis is still working for his father. Some sources say Francis was south of town and as he passed a crumbling abandoned Benedictine church, stopped in to pray. The church was called San Damiano, and Francis would have passed it many times on errands to check his father's properties. Abandoned and in a state of collapse, the church was unattended except for the intermittent presence of an old Benedictine priest. (The Benedictines had abandoned decrepit churches all over Umbria.)

An old wooden Byzantine image of the crucifix survived the decay and hung silently over what remained of the altar. Byzantine art developed around the sixth century as a kind of language, an icon that facilitated worship. These crosses were, and are, intended to draw the worshipper into contemplation—to instruct the illiterate and serve as a vibrant visual reminder of the exalted divinity of Christ. The cross in San Damiano represents the earliest period of such painted crosses, called Romanesque. In addition to the Christ, other figures appear, including, to Jesus' left, Saint John and Mary, and, to his right, Mary, Martha, and a centurion. Also present are Roman soldiers, angels, and a small rooster, the latter of which was discovered when the crucifix was cleaned in 1938. At the top, the resurrected Christ is surrounded by angels under the protecting hand of God.

In *First Life* Thomas of Celano says that Francis "discovered a certain church along the way that had been built of old in honor of Saint Damian, but which was now threatening to collapse because it was so old." In his *Second Life* he embellishes: "Changed in heart and soon to be changed in body too, he was walking one day near the church of Saint Damian. . . . [T]he painted image of Christ crucified moved its lips and spoke. Calling him by name it said, 'Francis, go, repair my house which, as you see, is falling completely into ruin.'"

Bonaventure avoids the moving lips, but adds that Francis "knelt in prayer before a painted image of the Crucified and heard a voice coming from the cross and telling him three times, 'Francis, go repair my house. You see it is falling down.'" (One historian told me, "There wasn't a crucifix in the thirteenth century that didn't speak.")

In his typical rush to heed the call, Francis went straight to his father's shop, took bolts of linens and a horse, and sold them at the market center of Foligno—including the horse. Then he returned to San Damiano and handed over the money to the priest to undertake necessary repairs.

But the priest had heard the rumors about the flamboyant son of Pietro Bernadone, and he knew well Pietro's reputation as a hardheaded, tightfisted businessman. "The priest was astounded and surprised at this sudden conversion," writes Thomas. "Because he thought he was being mocked, he refused to keep the money."[1] Francis refused to take it back. Instead, he tossed the money sack onto a windowsill in the church—and there it sat.

When Francis' father discovered his deficits in inventory (not to mention his missing horse), he went to the town officials and reported that money and goods had been stolen—by his son. Pietro appealed to them to use the force of law to compel Francis to return them. But the town officials refused to take the case, since the money

bag was sitting in a church. This made it a "church matter," independent of the authority of the *comune*. In the
meantime, Francis had become an oblate under the
guardianship of the frail old priest at San Damiano. (An
oblate is one who has surrendered himself to God and
thus comes under the protection of the Church.) Francis
had asked that "he might be allowed to stay for the Lord's
sake,"[2] and this left the priest no choice, given the sometimes inconvenient obligation of the church to shelter
refugees. The old priest put Francis in an underground
church chamber that had been built during Roman times
and had been used by soldiers as a place to worship and
make sacrifices to the goddess Mitre. While Francis was
there, his yet-unnamed friend brought him food and town
news.[3]

But the effrontery of Francis' taking linens and a horse
and selling them in Foligno threw Pietro into a rage. Feeling legally wronged and personally betrayed, he went after
his son—not simply to retrieve the money but also to denounce him publicly and show the community that Pietro
renounced his son's bad choices.

Francis had created a thorny problem for everyone involved. Because of his having become an oblate under the
guardianship of the Church, he no longer remained under
the jurisdiction of his family—or, for that matter, the civil
government. But Pietro was hot blooded and would stop at
nothing—indeed did stop at nothing—to get his son back
under his control. Word of Pietro's rage and intent got

around Assisi (as it tends to do in small towns), and Francis' special friend warned him of the impending crisis. So Francis burrowed himself in his underground hiding chamber. He did not want to be found by his father.

But there in his hideout, Francis felt abandoned by all but this special friend, who, in defiance of public sentiment, stayed true. The sources never identify this person. We know only that when all had abandoned Francis, this person proved more devoted. This solidarity and devotion will emerge again later in Francis' life from a special friend who, like this one, defied public sentiment to stay true to his ideals. The latter is certainly Clare—who, I believe, was likewise the friend in attendance to him during this troubled time.

In addition to praying and fasting, Francis spent many hours weeping. "Estranged is he in the city that was once his," wrote the poet Henri d'Avranches. "His true friends are sad; his false friends are smiling":

Nor will you say he is mistaken; rather will you say he is mad.
Not a friend of his spares him disparagement; all declare
him insane,
some think he drank of the poppy
of Lethe, some that he tasted slick brain-dulling hemlock
by infernal furies or else that he lacked the use of reason.
Some also said he was never cured, as he ought, from that
fever,
but that rear-chamber frenzy was begun, as fluids are fetched
up to the brains by the violent beat of his heart.[4]

Francis spent a whole month hiding underground, without coming out. He "grew used to prayer, for which he was free, and to fasting, in which he had no choice."[5]

And yet "grace from on high accompanies the wretch on his way," says the poet. In time Francis reproached himself for cowardice and left the cave to face his father. In the late fall of 1206 Francis entered Assisi's town center. The man who in earlier days had ridden high on his horse and made proclamations about becoming a prince and marrying the most beautiful woman in the world had become the object of ridicule by the hometown crowd. The writer of *Three Companions* tells of Francis' reentry into the world: "Those who knew him earlier, seeing him now, reproached him harshly. Shouting that he was insane and out of his mind, they threw mud from the streets and stones at him. For they saw him so changed from his earlier ways they blamed everything he did on starvation and madness."[6] They shoved him, grabbed him, picked up handfuls of mud, and hurled sticks at him.

The ruckus soon reached the ears of Pietro Bernadone. When he heard the name of his lunatic son associated with it, he determined he could endure no more. Having already suffered indignity and embarrassment because of his son's outlandish judgments, Pietro made his way through the mob and grabbed Francis, pulling and shaking him. According to a law in Assisi, "dissipaters" could be imprisoned upon the request of two relatives. Or as in other Italian towns, the father alone could send to prison a son who had squandered family assets—no matter whether the son was "of age" or still under the father's guardianship. A father could also fetter such a son in the family house, though he was obliged by the statutes to give his prisoner food. Many families maintained private prisons in their houses.[7]

Pietro "pounced on Francis like a wolf on a lamb and, glaring at him fiercely and savagely, he grabbed him and shamelessly dragged him home."[8] The writer of the *Three Companions* says that after Pietro "heard that the townspeople had done such things to him, he instantly arose to look for him, not to free him, but rather to destroy him. With no restraint, and glaring at him wild-eyed and savagely, he mercilessly took him in tow. Confining him to home and locking him up in a dark prison for several days, he strove, by words and blows, to turn his spirit."[9]

Shortly thereafter, business summoned Pietro to France. While he was gone, Pica promptly freed her son, who returned to the church at San Damiano. It was the last time Pica's involvement in the life of her son is mentioned in any record.

When Pietro returned, he was predictably incensed to discover that his wife had freed the prisoner. He beat her, too, but finally conceded he had no power over the situation. Thus he undertook legal proceedings for a public trial before the consuls. Bringing formal criminal charges against his son, Pietro accused Francis of theft and demanded restitution. He made it clear that he intended to disinherit Francis and have him banished from the city.

Although statutes prohibited authorities from intervening in family disputes unless loss of life or of limb was involved, the law did give a father the legal right to banish or imprison a child for "failure to obey." Francis had been guilty of that more than once in his youth.

Winter drew near. This particular year, 1206, was recorded as having had excessively heavy snowfalls. The Spoleto valley and the cap of Mount Subasio would have been shrouded in white when the messenger arrived at San Damiano on behalf of Pietro Bernadone and the town consuls. "Francesco di Pietro Bernadone," the messenger announced, "be it known to everyone that you, by order of the consuls, are to be accused and tried." The crier would have repeated the announcement a second and third time. Then the messenger would have handed Francis the document (a summons) claiming that according to the statutes Francis bore the legal obligation to appear for a trial.

But, being well versed in the ways of the world, Francis rebutted the summons. In effect, he said that the summons did not concern him, because he was an oblate under the protection of the Church. He was therefore exempt from the authority of the state. The exemption left the consuls in a difficult position. In his role as an oblate, Francis now could be considered subject only to the authority of the Church and the local bishop. This took the matter out of the hands of the magistrates.

Nevertheless, not long after the first messenger a second messenger arrived—this one from the bishop's palace. He issued Francis an order to appear at the church of Santa Maria Maggiore for a trial under the authority of the Church. This time Francis said, "I will appear before the lord bishop, because he is the father and lord of souls."[10]

The trial, with Assisi's Bishop Guido presiding, took place on a morning in March 1207, the snow still capping the mountain. It is not clear where on the bishop's premises it was held or if it was public. A fresco in Giotto's Franciscan cycle in the Basilica of San Francesco (the visual interpretation of Bonaventure's biography) depicts the episode as having taken place outside in the purview of any who wanted to watch. The *Three Companions* also suggests the presence of outsiders. If it was public, many friends from Francis' youth would have been there, along with neighbors and business associates, and certainly Clare. In any case, Pietro would have stood front and center, since he brought the charges. It is not known if Pica attended. The bishop, with his miter on his head and wearing a blue velvet mantle, would have rung a bell to begin the proceedings.

Pietro would have spoken first, repeating the accusations of theft against his son and his desire to extricate Francis from the family inheritance. He no doubt added commentary about his indignation at the hypocrisy of his son, now in rags and hiding in churches to avoid answering for his crime. In the end, Pietro's cruelty won sympathy for Francis

among the witnesses. And Bishop Guido addressed the de-
fendant with these words:

"Your father is infuriated and extremely scandalized.
If you wish to serve God, return to him the money
you have, because God does not want you to spend
money unjustly acquired on the work of the church.
[Your father's] anger will abate when he gets the
money back. My son, have confidence in the Lord
and act courageously. Do not be afraid, for he will be
your help and will abundantly provide you with whatever is necessary for the work of his church."[11]

Francis scripted the moment as only Francis could.

"My Lord, I will gladly give back not only the money
acquired from his things, but even all my clothes."
And going into one of the bishop's rooms, he took
off all his clothes, and, putting the money on top of
them, came out naked before the bishop, his father,
and all the bystanders, and said: "Listen to me, all of
you, and understand. Until now I have called Pietro
di Bernadone my father. But, because I have proposed to serve God, I return to him the money on
account of which he was so upset, and also all the
clothing which is his, wanting to say from now on:
'Our Father who is in heaven,' and not 'My father,
Pietro di Bernadone.'"[12]

A fresco by Giotto in the upper basilica of San Francesco depicting Francis' renunciation of his father. Bishop Guido is covering Francis' nakedness.

Even Pietro was silenced. As a result of this simple devastating act, Francis' father "rose up burning with grief and anger and he gathered up the garments and money and carried them home." Guido, equally stunned, removed his blue velvet mantle to cover the shivering boy.

Beginnings

Wearing an old tunic given to him by a local farmer, Francis left Assisi that day, heading north for the nearby city of Gubbio. He knew the path well. On he went, his spirits high after his decisive break from his old life in the drama at the bishop's hearing. While weaving his way through forests, mountain escarpments, and along the waters of the River Chiagio, he sang, loudly in French, as he so loved to do. Then bandits accosted him. The legends suggest his singing provoked it. The robbers asked who he was, and Francis answered in the spirit of the troubadours: "I am a herald of the Great King. What is that to you?"[1] Whereupon they beat him up, stripped him of the one cloak he possessed, and threw him in a ditch.

This put off his plans to reach Gubbio. Eventually he happened upon an old castle that belonged to a Benedictine monastery in a town called Valfábbrica, just north of Assisi, along the riverbank. The order's founder, Benedict, was born in Norcia, Umbria, in A.D. 480, and had left his imprint throughout the region. He had been a Roman noble who despaired over the dissolute way of life he experienced during his years of study in Rome. Leaving the city and exchanging that worldly existence for a life of reflection, penitence, and prayer, by 529 Benedict had won a following and unintentionally begun an order that was to shape the religious landscape of the Middle Ages. Benedict's teachings emphasized finding God in the ordinary circumstances of daily life, thus introducing the then-alien concept of the dignity of manual labor. The Benedictines harnessed rivers by building dams and dikes, and tamed the land to make it arable and farmable. Benedict also instituted a regimen of praying several times a day at specific hours, a practice called the Daily Office, which Francis faithfully adopted. The Benedictines, being rich in land and castles, owned monasteries and little churches throughout Umbria. By the time Francis was knocking at the gate of the monastery in Valfábbrica, the Benedictine Order had become strong, well established, and entrenched in its social standing. Francis took comfort in his hope that the brothers would take him in and give him refuge. He knocked, calling a second and a third time. Finally one of the brothers loosened the chains and let him in.

The monastery at Valfábbrica had lent military aid in Assisi's battle against Perugia at Collestrada in 1202 and had
been equally humiliated. They thus harbored wariness of
strangers and an underlying feeling of resentment against
unknown intruders. It happened that on the night Francis
arrived, the River Chiagio was rising—it was well known
for fierce and unpredictable flooding—and the brothers
were very distracted. So when this vagabond showed up at
their door beat up, cold, and naked (again), they saw him
as just another mouth to feed—and they had problems
enough already. Giving him a little bread and something
with which to cover himself, they told him he could sleep
in a corner of the kitchen. For the remainder of his brief
stay there, Francis was treated disparagingly. All the while,
he earned his keep holding forth on kitchen duty, splitting
wood, washing dishes, sweeping floors, stoking the fire, and
cleaning dung.[2]

He was understandably disillusioned. When the river
receded and the roads became passable, Francis left for
Gubbio, where he intended to visit an old friend.

* * * * * * * * * * * *

Like Assisi, Gubbio spills down the slope of a mountain. It
was a steeply fortressed town, built into a crag in the stone
and guarded by multiple forbidding towers. Throughout the
Middle Ages Assisi and Gubbio had shared long-standing
goodwill because of their geographic proximity—and their
common hatred for Perugia.

In Gubbio, Francis planned to visit his friend Federico Spadalunga ("Frederick Long-sword"), who had fought side by side with him at Collestrada. The two felt the unique camaraderie shared between fellow men of arms, and Spadalunga gladly welcomed Francis into his home, shocked though he was to see him so disheveled. He had known him only as a fierce and courageous warrior. Federico gave Francis a tunic and commended him to his companions in town, who welcomed him as the warrior friend of their hometown hero Spadalunga. Francis did his best to explain the change that had overtaken him—why he had renounced his former way of life to serve God and live in poverty. They didn't have a clue as to what he was talking about. They were Crusaders. In their minds the Holy Mother Church could not possibly be sustained without military might, particularly in an age when the pope and the emperor remained at odds and the holy sites in Jerusalem had fallen to the Saracens. They liked Francis. Yet ultimately Federico's friends in Gubbio paid him no mind.[3]

As in Valfábbrica, Francis felt isolated and disillusioned. He found himself missing home—the sunsets over the valley, the breeze off Mount Subasio, the tranquility of the olive groves along the hillsides. Thinking back to San Damiano, his "second home" during the struggles with his father, Francis decided that the time had come—the time to answer the vision he had received about rebuilding that old church. Soon, taking leave of his friend Spadalunga, a newly committed Francis began the slow trip back down the ridge toward home.

"He returned to San Damiano, gay and full of fervor, clothed in the hermit's garment," writes the author of *Three Companions*, "and comforted the priest of that church with the same words with which the bishop had comforted him [that God would provide funds to rebuild]."[4] Clare would become one source for such provisions.

The first work he undertook upon his return to Assisi was the overdue labor of rebuilding the ruined church of San Damiano. With no benefactors in sight, Francis worked amid the ruins calling out in French, begging for stones from passersby. Many people mocked him as a madman. Others were moved to tears "seeing how quickly he had come from such pleasure and worldly vanity to such an intoxication of divine love."[5] Francis paid no heed to ridicule. He had exchanged a life of extravagance for the habit of a hermit and the scorn heaped on beggars, and he did not shrink back. Francis would not abide idleness and demanded of himself and those who would later follow him that they work for whatever alms they might receive. Their payment was never to be in the form of money (unless it was intended to be used to help lepers) but in the form of food or other sustenance. When work was impossible because of illness or some other constraint, then asking for alms outright was permissible in exchange "for the love of God." Begging, in his mind, demonstrated assurance in the generosity of others, who, he felt confident, would give to him under the holy influence of God. When Francis rendered to the giver in return, "the love of God," it was, in his mind, more than a fair exchange. He refused to own anything or procure security of any kind, opting instead to trust God, who freely gives all necessities through the bounty of the earth and the generosity of the human spirit. Gratefully accepting whatever the world gave him, Francis trusted God for bread sufficient for the day, nothing more.[6] His choice of poverty, like a troubadour song, was an announcement of God's fidelity. He deemed beggars to be witnesses of God's presence upon the earth. "Brother, as long as you see a poor person, a mirror of the Lord and his poor Mother is placed before you. Likewise in the sick, look closely for the infirmities which He accepted," he said. "The great Almsgiver will accuse me of theft if I do not give what I have to someone in greater need."[7]

With a glad spirit, and with songs like those of the troubadours, Francis begged for stones to rebuild San Damiano. He had not started to command the following that in time would mark the birth of his religious order. But his convictions about poverty, and his example, were forging a curious narrative that began to define Francis' new vocation as a "religious."

Rebuilding San Damiano, Francis "did not know clearly what was to happen to him."[8] Yet he knew he intended for the building to become a home for religious women. "While laboring with others in that work, he used to cry to passers-by in a loud voice, filled with joy, saying in French:

'Come and help me in the work of the church of San Damiano which, in the future, will be a monastery of ladies through whose fame and life our heavenly Father will be glorified.'"[9] Francis "completed it in a short time,"[10] and a few years later Clare moved in, eventually joined by her sister, some blood relatives, and other women. Clare describes the episode in her *Testament*, written shortly before her death:

> While building the church of San Damiano, where he was totally visited by divine consolation and impelled to abandon the world, completely through great joy and the enlightenment of the Holy Spirit, the holy man made a prophecy about us that the Lord later fulfilled. Climbing the wall of that church, he shouted in French to some poor people who were standing nearby: "Come and help me in the work on the monastery of San Damiano, because there will as yet be ladies here who will glorify our heavenly Father."[11]

After finishing San Damiano, Francis promptly began work on two more ruined churches, one called San Pietro della Spina (not to be confused with the commanding tenth-century Church of San Pietro near Assisi's low eastern gate) and another called the Portiuncula, which would become his beloved home and the seat of the blossoming order. He carried a staff, wore the habit of a hermit, with shoes on his feet and a leather belt. He had not yet assumed the definitive garb (stricter and with fewer accoutrements) that would become the hallmark of the Friars Minor. Clare was still living with her family and assisting Francis' efforts rebuilding the Portiuncula by means of financial help.

In time, Francis' building activity began to attract attention. Some in his hometown had dismissed him as mad. Others, moved by his humility, tenacity, and happiness in the face of poverty and ridicule, had felt sympathy for him. Inevitably, he began to be approached by some of Assisi's citizens who had become curious about his work. The first to inquire was a wealthy man of arms named Bernard of Quintavalle, a respected and learned member of the *maggiore*.[12] Bernard held degrees in civil and canon law, and many of the leaders in Assisi's government frequently solicited his advice. He owned a home in Assisi not far from Francis' family home, was approximately the same age as Francis, and probably had fought with him in battle. He would not have been numbered among the rabble who crowned Francis *dominus* in earlier days, for Bernard was known to have led a measured and respectable civic life. He watched from a distance as surprising changes overtook the erstwhile party-loving son of Pietro Bernadone, and he couldn't make sense of them. He harbored questions. More than once, Bernard invited Francis to stay in his home in Assisi, and Francis gladly accepted. Bernard understood that the townspeople were calling him crazy, yet during these intimate conversations Francis' bearing was sound and he expressed himself cogently. This fired the imagination of this respected citizen and aroused desires he couldn't put a finger on.

The legends say that one night when Francis was staying in Bernard's home, his host found him not sleeping but praying. This, in Bernard's mind, consummated the mounting evidence that Francis' change was authentic and his convictions worthy to be trusted. He resolved to join Francis in the life of a penitent.

Bernard was laden with properties in and around Assisi. He asked Francis what to do about it: "If someone had received from his master property entrusted to his care, be it much or little, and had had possession of it for many years, and now wanted to keep it no longer, what would be the best way to act in such a case?" Francis said, "Give it back to him of whom he had received it."

Bernard's predicament demanded legal maneuvering. So together he and Francis consulted a man of law in Assisi, a prominent citizen named Peter of Catanio. Peter's family, like Bernard's, was well respected. He lived in the neighborhood of the Cathedral of San Rufino among the other nobility (where Clare also lived). Peter, too, had been baffled by Francis' strange new allegiance, and was even more baffled now that Bernard of Quintavalle had embraced it. The three men shared many probing conversations. In time, Peter joined them in their desire to live the penitent life, and together they explored how to appropriate it given their current station. The three set out together to the Church of San Nicolo—next door to Francis' childhood home—where Francis knew the priest. The priest read verses from Matthew's Gospel (19:21): "If you seek perfection, go, sell your possessions, and give to the poor. Take nothing on the way. If a man wishes to come after me, he must deny his very self."[13] Francis concluded that this was the answer. He told Peter and Bernard to "go and fulfill everything you have heard."

The other townspeople were confounded. How could the lunatic son of Pietro Bernadone persuade two of the commune's wisest, most respected, most educated, and most heroic citizens to undertake this course of madness? When it had been only Francis begging for alms and stones in exchange for the love of God, they could dismiss the behavior as his own version of madness. But his oddities had now been validated by two outstanding citizens who had similarly renounced society and rank.

The Feast of San Giorgio, the patron saint of Francis' boyhood school, occasioned the coming of a third follower to join his small band. His name was Giles, a young man of heroic virtue who, like Francis, had longed for the glory of knighthood. In late April the town was preparing for its usual festivities related to the feast day, including a joust and other contests that Giles hoped would give him an opportunity for valor. Nevertheless, he, along with all citizens of Assisi, had heard gossip about Francis. Even more alarming, he had heard that the great man of arms Bernard of Quintavalle, along with Peter of Catanio, had joined Francis' ranks. Giles had known that Francis once aspired to knighthood; he knew as well that San Giorgio himself claimed a kind of knighthood that served a higher king. All knew the portion of the tale recounting how San Giorgio gave to the poor the noble horse that he had been riding, and his knight's armor, which was nobly and richly decorated, for the love of God.

At once enamored and confused, the young man set about looking for Francis to try to reconcile the contradiction. He meandered through the oak forests and cypress groves in the valley below Assisi near the Portiuncula, where he knew Francis was staying. In time Giles spied Francis walking toward the little church. Longing for knighthood in the likeness of San Giorgio, and embracing the code of chivalry that attended it, he knelt before Francis as a would-be knight would bow before his king. Francis recognized the gesture. Keeping with the code, Francis exhorted Giles the way a king would a knight: "Remain strong in every trial and firm and constant in the vocation to which he has been called by God."[14]

Giles' first test to knighthood came immediately. He and the other brothers were walking toward town, where they planned to get Giles some sackcloth for a tunic. An old woman approached asking for alms. Between them they had no money, though Giles still wore his mantle of blue satin. Francis turned to him and urged him "for the love of God," to give his mantle to this poor woman.

By 1208 or early 1209, then, a handful of Assisi's noble citizens had voluntarily assumed beggars' garb in order to

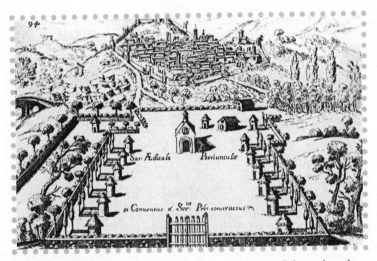

The Portiuncula in the valley below Assisi, home of the order when Francis lived, as it would have looked during his time. (Print of painting of Francesco Providone, seventeenth century.)

follow Francis. Eventually known as Assisi's "penitents," they included, among others, Clare's noble cousin Rufino; a troubadour poet known as Pacifico, King of Verse (and crowned poet laureate of the empire by Emperor Frederick II); a handsome and eloquent personality named Masseo, who once harbored jealousy toward Francis; and a knight and minstrel named Angelo, from the great house of Tancredo, a powerful family in Assisi.[15] Leo, who joined the order by 1211, became Francis' scribe, traveling companion, confessor, and his closest and most trusted friend. Before then, Leo may have served the brothers in his capacity as an ordained priest to say the mass. Francis wanted the offices read daily and the mass celebrated everywhere he went.

And Francis was always going somewhere. That meant he was obliged to bring a member of the clergy with him to carry the chalice and breviary, to consecrate the host and read the lesson. Along with everything else, Leo also served as Francis' priest.[16]

At the time when these earliest companions had renounced rank to join Francis, he "was still altogether ignorant of how things would turn out for him and his new-found brothers."[17] This is when, in 1209, Francis decided the time had come to write a rule—that is, a governing document for a religious order.

Reversal

The organizing principle of society in Francis' day was the Church. Picture a series of concentric circles with the pope as the bull's eye at the center. The ring around the pope consisted of cardinals, bishops, and other overlords. In the next ring were the clerics and laics. Finally there was the outer ring—the poor, the beggars, and others destined to live out their days in isolation and beset by society's intolerance, most pointedly, the lepers.

Incoming patients at every leprosy hospital were commanded by the priest to take a vow. Upon entering, the patient bowed before the altar as the local priest proclaimed:

Dear poor little man of good God, by means of great sadness and tribulation of sickness, of leprosy, and of many other miseries, one gains the kingdom of heaven where there is no sickness or sorrow and all is pure and white, without stain, more brilliant than the sun. You will go there, if it pleases God. In the meantime, be a good Christian, bear with patience this adversity and God will be merciful to you.

My brother, the separation has to do only with your body. As for the spirit, which is more important, you are still as you were before, a participant in the prayers of our Holy Mother Church. Charitable men will provide for your lesser needs and God will never abandon you. Take care of yourself and have patience. God is with you. Amen.

The priest then sprinkled dirt over the leper's head. "Die to the world, be born again in God," the priest intoned. "O Jesus my Redeemer, who made me of earth and clothed me with a body, make me to rise again in the new day." Then he rendered final instructions:

In the name of the Father, the Son, and the Holy Spirit:

My brother, take this cloak and put it on as a sign of humility and never leave here without it.

Take this flask. Put in it what will be given you to drink, and under penalty of disobedience I forbid you to drink from the rivers, from the springs, from the wells.

Take these gloves. You are forbidden to touch anything with your bare hands that is not yours.

If, while walking about, should you meet someone who wishes to talk to you, I forbid you to reply before you put yourself against the wind.

You are forbidden to be with any woman who is not of your family. You are forbidden to touch young people or to offer them anything. And from eating from anything but your own leper's bowl; and from entering churches or rectories, and from going to fairs, to mills, and to markets; and from walking through narrow streets where those who meet you cannot avoid you.

Take this tentennella [rattle]; carry it always with you. Sound it to warn others of your presence.

To which the leper then responded: "Here is my perpetual resting place. Here I shall live. This is my vow."[1]

Francis, however, loved the lepers and desired to identify with them in poverty. This was the mandate of his rule. In it he articulated a literal application of Jesus' words in the Gospel to sell all possessions and serve the poor. The short document Francis composed in 1209 known as the "primitive rule" (it is now lost) was written "in simple language including words from the holy gospel" and in effect turned the concentric circles inside out. The rule by implication put lepers and other outcasts at the center, reversing the prevailing hierarchical order governed by the Church. Francis' identity with the social fringe could have been seen as tantamount to a call to revolution against the Church—indeed some of his later followers interpreted his teachings this way. But in truth the only revolt Francis had in mind was to invite the outcast in from his isolation on the edges and place him front and center in the family of God. Francis took seriously his identity with the lepers and demanded that all his brothers likewise embrace it.[2]

Francis' aim was to take his rule to be confirmed by the supreme authority, the pope. So, the following summer, Francis and his small band set out for Rome to meet the pontiff with the hope and intention to gain papal approval to live the life outlined in the short rule. In those days heresies with a penitential bent were developing rapidly, and the Church was winnowing them out as much as possible. Francis wanted papal approval for his infant order so that it would be clear beyond any doubt that what he proposed was not heretical or in violation of the orthodox teachings of the Gospel. On the contrary, he was asking the Church to affirm that his rule was in fact a positive and authentic assertion of Christ's teaching. But at the same time, the only way he could gain credibility and the moral authority to teach was to win the approval of the sole governing authority of all things Christian—the pope himself. This meant that the Curia had a very fine needle to thread.

* * * * * * * * * * *

Once in Rome, Francis and his brothers met Assisi's Bishop Guido, the same bishop who just two years before had covered a naked, shivering Francis with his mantle. Guido had a friend in the Curia, a Cardinal Giovanni, who hosted Francis and his entourage. Because of the Curia's suspicion of heresies, the cardinal urged Francis to adopt a preexisting rule rather than solicit permission to start a new order. But Francis wouldn't hear of it. Thomas of Celano notes that "as much as he could, he humbly refused his urging." He "stuck firmly to what he had begun and modestly refused to agree to suggestions of this sort."[3] Cardinal Giovanni sympathized, and Francis prevailed. The cardinal promised to present Francis' request to the Curia and to Pope Innocent III.

Before becoming pope, Innocent III had been John Lothar, count of Segni. He was "small of stature, but handsome; extremely learned in trivium and quadrivium."[4] He had studied theology in Paris and law in Bologna and was described as having surpassed all in his knowledge of theology. He "possessed an extremely quick and brilliant mind; was very eloquent, fluent, and quick of tongue, with a sonorous voice that can be heard and understood by all, even if the tone is low."[5]

Elected to the papacy in January 1198 and taking the name Innocent III, he promptly undertook a vigorous effort to strengthen the Church's position politically. Innocent III zealously defended the position of the Church as guide and governor of all human activity and went to work to bend all kingdoms to that end. He was bold. Some say he was brazen. By the time Francis and his ragtag humble following came face-to-face with Innocent, the pope had established dominion over most of central and southern Italy and had secured the Holy See (the central government of the Catholic Church) as the political seat of John, king of England; Pietro II, king of Aragon; Kaloyan, king of Bulgaria; Ottokar, king of Bohemia; Alphonso IX, king of Leòn (in Spain); and various Cilican kingdoms of Armenia.[6]

Innocent was tolerant of penitential movements and, according to one friar I spoke with, "was more spiritual than other popes." He understood the advantage of bringing penitents under the obedience of the Church, and to that end was willing to concede certain points—poverty, for example—in exchange for a profession of allegiance to the Church. Under his guidance two of Catholicism's most significant mendicant orders were born and flourished, the Franciscans and the Dominicans.

It is evident and indeed predictable that Innocent was not initially convinced by Francis' plea for approval of his simple rule. Thomas's *Second Life* said Innocent told Francis to go and pray.[7] Bonaventure's version is less sublime. He says the initial visit with the pope went badly: "He knew nothing about the saint and so he sent him away indignantly."[8]

Regardless, Francis got another hearing, and his request fueled squabbling in the Curia. Some felt his claims to poverty were too severe and would be impossible for any order to embrace in a sustainable way. To this charge Francis replied that renunciation was a gift from Christ, so it did not depend upon man's abilities or weakness. "The King of Kings himself will provide for all the sons he wills to raise up through me because, if he cares for strangers, he will also do so for his own children."[9] Others in the Curia said his rule smacked too much of heretics who made similar claims of renunciation, such as the Catharists and the Waldensians.[10] Yet Francis had made it humbly but forcefully clear that he was simply asking that he and his fraternity be allowed to live out the Gospel freely as they understood it from Jesus himself—and that they be able to do so without interference from the Church.

Bishop Guido's friend Cardinal Giovanni articulated the Curia's predicament: "We must be careful. If we refuse this beggarman's request because it is new or too difficult we may be sinning against Christ's Gospel, because he is only asking us to approve a form of Gospel life. Anyone who says that a vow to live according to the perfection of the Gospel contains something new or unreasonable or too difficult is guilty of blasphemy against Christ, the author of the Gospel."[11]

After his meeting with Francis, Innocent III had a dream. He saw the Basilica of St. John Lateran—the cathedral in Rome that served as the official ecclesiastical seat of the pope. The towers creaked and the walls cracked as the pope looked on helplessly. He then saw a small man dressed as a peasant, barefoot and with a rope about his waist, coming toward the Lateran piazza. The little man went to the falling church and stood beside one of the crumbling walls and shouldered it until it stood erect. Innocent perceived the dream to be an omen. He became convinced that the little man who shouldered the falling palace was the mendicant peasant who had come asking for his blessing. Seeing Francis the next time, "he embraced Francis and approved the Rule he had written and gave him permission to preach penance to all."[12] Francis described the episode in his *Testament* by stating dryly, "his holiness the Pope confirmed [the rule] for me." Innocent III orally approved Francis' first short rule, known then as *Propositum vitae*, and thus the new Order of the Friars Minor ("lesser brothers") was born. Cardinal Giovanni gave Francis and his brothers the tonsure—the shaved portion at the crown of the head that signaled the pope's permission to preach—and Francis went back to Assisi, where he "began to speak out more boldly owing to the apostolic authority he had been granted."

In turn the Church benefited from Francis' "felicitous leadership of both sexes,"[13] which brings us back to Clare.

Gentle Fire

The time arrived when Clare chose the one she would marry—when she gave flight to her will. The early sources create a stunning, sometimes shocking, depiction of the dramatic events surrounding Clare's choice to leave her family and follow Francis. It was an event that sent tremors through Assisi at the time, and its impact remains to this day.

The noblewomen of the house of Offreduccio attended mass together on that Palm Sunday in March, sometime between the years 1210 and 1212. Clare would have been sitting on the bench with her sisters and mother, wearing her most elegant attire. Palm Sunday, celebrated the week before Resurrection Sunday, highlighted the occasion of Jesus' final entrance into Jerusalem before his death, when crowds turned out to greet him with palm fronds. It was a festive occasion on which women showed off their most extravagant fashions.

In churches throughout the world both then and now, worshippers on Palm Sunday rise from their seats to go to the altar and receive a palm, which they raise in memory of the grand entrance of Jesus into Jerusalem. On this particular day, however, while her mother and sisters advanced to the altar, one young worshipper remained in her place weeping. The presiding bishop, Guido (the same priest who had covered Francis with his cloak), took note of the disconsolate Clare alone on the bench, tears tracking down her cheeks. Departing from church protocol, he left the platform and went to her to extend a palm branch, which she accepted.[1] But the reason for her tears did not abate.

That night, after dark, Clare put on her walking shoes and cloaked herself to face the bracing night winds off Mount Subasio. Loosening the iron bolt from a hidden door in the family home, known as the death door (from which bodies of deceased family members would be removed from the home for burial), she then slipped away from her childhood home, never to return.

"Embarking on her long-desired flight," as one source described it, Clare would have skirted through Assisi's dimly lit alleys to escape through the southern gate that opened on to the plain below town, where Francis awaited her.

Clare's blood sister Beatrice, who would later join her in penitential vows, attested in the testimonies related to

Clare's canonization investigation that her sister left the family at the urging of Francis. "He went to her many times, so that the virgin Clare acquiesced, renounced the world and all earthly things and went to serve God as soon as she was able." Another witness, a knight of Assisi named Ugolino di Pietro Girardone, asserted that Francis' complicity in the episode was "public knowledge." "Clare entered religion through the preaching of Francis and his admonition." When Ugolino was asked how he knew that Francis had been the impetus behind Clare's flight, he said, "This was public knowledge and known by everyone."[2]

Francis, along with a few of his brothers, met Clare in the plain with torches and a plan. Exhausted, mud-splattered, and flushed, Clare followed him to his dwelling, the small church he had rebuilt called the Portiuncula. There he cut her hair.[3]

The following days would prove harrowing for Clare (and Francis). After her tonsure, Francis took her to a Benedictine convent called San Paolo, approximately four kilometers west of Assisi near the River Chiagio. She was to remain there temporarily under the protection of the sisters until Francis could secure her permanent dwelling.[4]

When light broke on Monday morning, Clare's family discovered that she was gone. Outraged, they dispatched knights and relatives to retrieve her—by force, if need be. Her sister Beatrice recounts that these emissaries went to the convent at San Paolo and attempted to drag Clare out. "Clare grabbed the altar cloths and uncovered her head,

showing them she was tonsured." With that, the family despaired of her and gave her up to Francis.

The commotion with the knights and relatives violated
the rules of asylum that had been granted to Benedictine
sisters, and the tumult compelled Francis to remove Clare
promptly from San Paolo. He then took her to another
convent, east of Assisi along the slope of Mount Subasio,
called Sant'Angelo di Panzo.

A little more than two weeks after her departure, Clare's
blood sister Catherine (later called Agnes) joined her
there. "The Legend of Saint Clare" notes, "The divine
majesty quickly gave her that first gift she so eagerly
sought"—her sister. "Embracing her with joy, [Clare] said,
'I thank God, most sweet sister, that he has heard my concern for you.'" "Legend" continues:

> The next day, hearing Agnes had gone off to Clare,
> twelve men, burning with anger and hiding outwardly
> their evil intent, ran to the place and pretended to
> make peaceful entrance. They turned to Agnes, since
> they had long ago lost hope of reclaiming Clare, and
> said, "Why have you come to this place? Get ready to
> return immediately." When she responded that she did
> not want to leave her sister Clare, one of the knights,
> without sparing blows and kicks, tried to drag her away
> by her hair, while the others pushed her and lifted her
> in their arms.[5]

According to "Legend," they carried Agnes along the slope of the mountain, still tearing her clothes and pulling out her hair, casting them aside along the path. Clare followed them, beseeching them on her sister's behalf, and finding her sister near death on the ground alongside the road. How (and if) Clare convinced them to leave her is not known. And no one knows how long she took to recover after being left along the road. In time, however, Francis tonsured her, too, and soon established Clare and her sister at the place he had intended for them all along—the small church he rebuilt called San Damiano. Thus with blows, wounds, tears, and blood, Clare's beatific life as a religious commenced.

Apart from the initial trauma of this episode, after the fact—and especially during the investigation for her canonization—one of the most contentious unresolved details about Clare's flight is the matter of her age at the time. It is a question made more confusing by the vague and inconsistent accounts afforded by her canonization witnesses. Clare's age is generally contentious because, first, there is no record of the date of her birth, and, second, it is widely assumed that she was much younger than Francis, so their friendship could be defined only as similar to that of a father and daughter. Nevertheless, the consensus of the witnesses suggests that Clare may have been older than has been widely accepted at the time she left home to join Francis. Moreover, it indicates that her age was a subject that was talked about within the convent.

Of the twenty witnesses examined under oath during the investigation for Clare's canonization, ten make reference to Clare's age at the time of her flight. Of these ten, only one speaks of it unambiguously. This would be witness number seventeen, Lady Bona, daughter of Guelfuccio of Assisi. The testimony reads: "At the time [Clare] entered Religion, she was a prudent young girl of eighteen years." When asked how she knew these things, Lady Bona replied that she "used to converse with her." Nine of the ten witnesses who addressed the question of Clare's age were less exacting. Witness number one, Pacifica di Guelfuccio of Assisi, said Clare "left the world about forty-two years" before her death. Witness number two, Benvenuta of Perugia, said of Clare's age upon leaving her family: "She was eighteen years old or so, according to what was said." Witness number six, Cecilia, daughter of Sir Gualtieri Cacciaguerra of Spoleto, said, "It could have been forty-three years or so that the Lady had been governing the sisters." Witness number eight, Sister Lucia of Rome, when asked how long Clare had been at the monastery, replied, "She had been there so long [I do] not remember." Witness number twelve, Clare's blood sister Beatrice, said that Clare "renounced the world and all earthly things and went to serve God as soon as she was able." When asked how many years ago that had taken place she said, "About forty-two years ago." Witness number thirteen, Sister Cristiana, daughter of Sir Bernardo da Suppo of Assisi, was asked the same question and replied, "It was forty-two years or a little more." When she was asked Clare's age at the time, she answered, "According to what was said, she was eighteen years old." Witness number eighteen, Lord Ranieri di Bernardo of Assisi, said the timing of her flight "was more than forty years ago," adding, "as quickly as possible she had her hair cut by Saint Francis." He said that "when [Clare's] relatives wanted to take her from San Paolo and bring her back to Assisi they could in no way persuade her because she did not want to go. She showed them her tonsured head. Thus they let her stay." Witness number nineteen, a man named Pietro di Damiano of Assisi (a neighbor), said "the young girl at that time [was] about seventeen or so," and witness number twenty, Ioanni di Ventura of Assisi, said Clare "could have been eighteen or so." The remaining witnesses make no mention of age or time sequencing related to Clare's departure.

Many of those who answered the age questions did so "according to what was said," which suggests that something was "being said" about how to address the question. Moreover, the nebulous and continuous qualifier "or so" leaves room to round the number up, as opposed to down. The implication is, Clare may have been older than "what was said." This could put Clare's age closer to Francis by at least a few years, which also carries the implication that their relationship would not, of necessity, have to have been defined in father-daughter terms.

Other interesting insights about Clare were also gleaned from these witnesses. Lady Bona said in her testimony that she had accompanied Clare on clandestine meetings with

Francis "so as not to be seen by her parents." Lady Bona also testified that "while she was still in the world"—before she fled her family—Clare "gave [me] a certain amount of money as a votive offering and directed [me] to carry it to those who were working on Saint Mary of the Portiuncula so that they would sustain the flesh." Sister Beatrice, Clare's actual sibling, added that Francis "went many times to preach to her" and that "Clare acquiesced to his preaching." Lord Ranieri di Bernardo of Assisi gives a fascinating, if humiliating, account admitting that he had been among her many suitors who had been decisively rebuffed. He described her as having "a beautiful face" and said that "many relatives begged her to accept [a suitor] as a husband." He himself "had many times asked her to be willing to consent to this," but "she did not even want to hear [me]."

In any case, Clare's age at her departure to join Francis is anything but clear. She was minimally in her late teens and possibly older. But this much, in sum, is known: She left to join Francis "as soon as she could."[6] She fled the night of Palm Sunday in secret and alone. She did so at the behest of Francis, who met her and cut her hair. He had made all necessary arrangements for temporary asylum. Upon discovering her disappearance, the family reacted with force, trying and failing to retrieve her. The episode was big news in town and more so because Clare's shocking behavior had been scripted by the one-time-profligate-turned-lunatic religious. Clare's sister Catherine/Agnes nearly died at the hands of relatives, but didn't. And she lived out the rest of her days with Clare.

The implications are many. Bishop Guido perceived Clare's emotions as she wept alone on the bench that Palm Sunday, and he broke protocol to approach and encourage her. This suggests that he might have understood the cause of her tears. He and Francis were known to have shared a close bond, and Guido had been intimately involved with all previous critical decisions relating to Francis' religious life. Since Francis deemed him the "guardian and protector of souls," it is unlikely that Francis and Clare would have executed so daring a plan without consulting the bishop. It is also probable that the complicated logistics of Clare's temporary lodging would have required his helpful intervention. In any case, that day as she sat by herself on the bench, Bishop Guido gave Clare his blessing. It can also be inferred that Clare's sister Catherine/Agnes had been privy to the plan—and probably knew that she herself would follow shortly thereafter. Catherine kept track of Clare after the latter's departure and knew precisely where to go (to Clare's second location at Sant'Angelo di Panzo). She also no doubt anticipated the ruckus it would cause when the time came for her to join her sister.

Clare desired her flight "for a long time," which suggests that plans had been in the making for a lengthy period before the event itself. She fled "as soon as she was able," which likewise suggests something precluded her going sooner. We have already noted that Francis worked on San Damiano early on after his conversion, with the intention of housing women there (before he thought to begin an order). Yet the church belonged to the Benedictines, and rebuilt by him or not, he had to secure the arrangement to "rent" it on a permanent basis, which may have complicated the timing. We now know that for a long time—probably years—before Clare's departure, Francis was "admonishing" her and "whispering in her ears of a sweet espousal with Christ,"[7] encouraging her to follow him. In the end, Francis chose the day she would flee and where she would go while she "committed herself thoroughly to the counsel of Francis, placing him, after God, as the guide of her journey."

So, "trembling with fear at the allurements of the flesh," she ran that night to join Francis, binding herself to his destiny. "Clare was not an ordinary young girl leaving her parents to enter monastic life," wrote biographer Marco Bartoli. "Nor was Francis a bishop—to whom the consecration of virgins was normally reserved. In fact, he was not even a priest but only a layman, and yet he took upon himself the right to consecrate Clare." Her life was in his hands.

Francis ultimately secured her lodging at San Damiano and "saw flourish inside a temple of the Spirit and outside, the work of his hands," wrote Henri d'Avranches. Thus, the writer added, Francis "brought his plan to a happy end."

The Round Table

Clare was deemed the lady of the castle, while Francis referred to his band of followers, officially known as the "lesser brothers," as his "Knights of the Round Table, who hide in deserted and remote places."[1] He wished both sisters and brothers to be a "new and humble" people who "distinguished themselves by their poverty and humility."[2] But upon his male companions he imposed and expected the code of chivalry: duty, dignity, self-sacrifice, and the rule of love.

In their early years Francis and his brothers were a motley band, still in their youth and sharing good humor. Even so, they were not without conflicts caused by relational dynamics, personal eccentricities, and spiritual struggles. They were sometimes bewildered, sometimes weak, other times heroic, always human, and for the most part devoted to Francis' version of perfect joy. They watched as he preached to birds, or preached naked, or preached without words. Brother Masseo, "a big man and handsome of body"[3]—who had said of Francis, "You aren't a handsome man, you aren't someone of great learning, you're not noble"—once asked him, "Why after you? Why after you? Why does all the world seem to be running after you and everyone seems to want to see you and hear you and obey you?"[4] Another time, after Francis had ordered Brother Rufino, Clare's cousin, to go to Assisi and preach naked before the people, Francis rebuked himself: "How can you, the son of Pietro Bernadone, you vile little wretch, order Brother Rufino, who is one of the noblest citizens of Assisi to go naked and preach to the people like a madman?" On another occasion, while praying in caves, Rufino was overtaken with the idea that Francis was a liar and that he himself was deceived in following him.[5] Even Brother Leo, Francis' closest and most devoted companion, at times harbored hidden questions. "Look—this man calls himself a very great sinner in public, and he came into the Order as an adult, and he is honored much by God, and yet in secret he never confesses carnal sin—can he be a virgin?"[6]

Masseo's jealousy, Rufino's doubt, and Leo's questions barely touch upon the spectrum of complex emotions experienced by those who followed and loved Francis.[7] The Friars Minor were a humble, sometimes eccentric band devoted to their leader. Yet Francis trumped them all in eccentricity and devotion. In answer to Brother Masseo's question, Francis responded:

Do you want to know why after me? You want to know why after me? You want to know why the whole world comes after me? I have this from those eyes of the Most High God, which gaze in every place on the good and the guilty. Since those most holy eyes have not seen among sinners anyone more vile, nor more incompetent, nor a greater sinner than me; to perform that marvelous work, which he intends to do, He has not found a more vile creature on the earth, and therefore He has chosen me.[8]

When Francis rebuked himself for humiliating Rufino in commanding him to preach naked, he did so not by retracting the command but by joining him in the humiliation: They preached naked together on "the nakedness and shame of the Passion of our Lord Jesus Christ."[9] ("Brother Leo very discreetly carried along the Saint's habit and Brother Rufino's too."[10]) And when Francis heard about Rufino's doubts, he went to him immediately. "Brother Rufino, whom have you believed? You should have known that he was the devil because he hardened your heart to everything that is good, for that is exactly his job. But the blessed Christ never hardens the heart of the faithful man but rather softens it." He told him the next time the devil assails him, he should "answer him confidently, 'Open your mouth and I will shit in it!'"[11]

As for Leo's questioning, Francis' tenderness toward Leo is depicted in an extant document written to him by Francis' own hand:

Brother Leo, health and peace from Brother Francis. I am speaking, my son, in this way—as a mother would—because I am putting everything we said on the road in this brief message and advice. If, afterwards, you need to come to me for counsel, I advise you thus: In whatever way it seems better to you to please the Lord God and to follow His footprint and poverty, do it with the blessing of the Lord God and my obedience. And if you need and want to come to me for the sake of your soul or for some consolation, Leo, come.[12]

• • • • • • • • • • • •

They were good knights, and Francis upheld their composite qualities as the picture of courtly devotion. To be a "good Lesser Brother," he said, one ought to possess

the faith and love of poverty which Brother Bernard most perfectly had; the simplicity and purity of Brother Leo; the courtly bearing of Brother Angelo; the friendly manner and common sense of Brother Masseo, together with his attractive and gracious eloquence; the mind raised in contemplation which Brother Giles had even to the highest perfection; the virtuous and constant prayer of Brother Rufino who, whatever he was doing, even sleeping, always prayed; the patience of Brother Juniper; the bodily and spiritual strength of Brother John of Lauds, who at that time in his robust body surpassed everyone; the charity of Brother Roger; the solicitude of Brother Lucidus who did not remain in any

A note written from Francis' hand
to encourage Brother Leo. In it he
tells Leo that if he needs to come
see him, "then, Leo, come."

place for a month, saying "*We do not have* a dwelling *here*
on earth, but in heaven.[13]

In the early days of the order, Francis traveled about on his
mission as an energetic mendicant friar. One early source in
particular, called the *Fioretti* (Little Flowers), offers a rich

compilation of anecdotes about Francis' religious life.[14] It is replete with references such as "when he was traveling on the road"; "standing by the bank of a broad river"; "traveling in Tuscany"; "they came to a village"; and "they went beyond the seas." Francis traveled (on foot) throughout Umbria to such places as Cannara, Bevagna, Montefalco, Spoleto, Monteluco, Gubbio, Orvieto, Perugia, Bologna, Cortona, and the Lake of Perugia (Lake Trasimeno), among many others. He traveled to city centers such as Siena, Florence, Rome, and Arezzo. He often retreated to his beloved solitary mountaintops, such as La Verna and Greccio. He walked south to Rieti and even farther, to Slavonia, the Marches of Trevisi, the Marches of Ancona, and Apulia. He made his way to Syria, Egypt, and possibly Jerusalem and Spain.

When he traveled, he was accompanied primarily by Brother Leo. Francis surpassed Leo in age by a few years—as youths Leo would have known Francis' brother, Angelo, better. But the two grew up in Assisi together, and they would have heard the same stories. They would have listened to tales of Arthur's knights, and of Picardy and Flanders in their battles for the commune. They would have heard the news of Saladin, the Saracen, taking Jerusalem. Leo would have seen Francis become first a soldier, then an invalid, and then a religious. Francis called Leo *Frate Pecorella di Dio,* "God's little lamb"—a nickname attributed to Leo for his well-known meekness and self-doubt, for which he continually sought the succor of his friend.

In their traveling, Leo scaled mountains with Francis and bounded with him through Assisi's labyrinth of alleys. He later watched as Francis grew weak with illness. When he could no longer negotiate mountains and alleys, Leo walked slowly alongside him. When Francis could no longer walk, Leo steadied him on a mule. When Francis could no longer ride, Leo carried him on his mat. And when at last his beloved friend raised weary arms to welcome Sister Death, it would be Leo who laid him naked on the ground.

Once, as they returned to Assisi after a journey, Francis had a conversation with Leo that both showed how his mind worked and laid bare his dependence on Leo—not only as a friend but as a sounding board and scribe, too. It also reveals Leo's patience. Francis said:

> Brother Leo, write this down. A messenger comes and says that all the masters of theology in Paris have joined the Order. Write: this is not true joy; also all the prelates beyond the mountains, archbishops and bishops, or the King of France and the King of England. Write: this is not true joy. Or that my friars have gone to the unbelievers and have converted all of them to the faith; or that I have so much grace from God that I heal the sick and perform many miracles. I tell you that true joy is not in all those things.
>
> Leo asks, "But what *is* true joy?"

Francis said, "This is joy: I am returning from Perugia and I am coming at night, in the dark. It is winter time and I am wet and muddy and so cold that icicles form at the edges of my habit and strike my legs and blood flows from the wounds. I come to the gate, covered with mud and cold and ice and, after I have knocked and called for a long time, a friar comes and asks: Who are you? I answer, 'Brother Francis.' And he says 'Go away. You can't come in.'

"And when I insist again, he replies: 'Go away. You are a simple and uneducated fellow. From now on don't stay with us any more. We are so many and so important that we don't need you.'

"I will stand at the gate and say: 'For the love of God, let me come in tonight.' And he answers, 'I won't.'

"I say that if I kept patience and was not upset—that, Brother Leo—is true joy and true virtue and the salvation of the soul."[15]

* * * * * * * * * * * *

The brothers were Francis' knights and Clare the lady of the castle. Thus, true to the code of chivalry, he promised her his devotion. "I desire and promise you personally and in the name of my friars," he wrote her, "that I will always have the same loving care and special solicitude for you as for them."[16]

In the early years of her life in the cloister, Clare made a request to share a meal with Francis, asking "several times to give her that consolation." But "Francis always refused to grant her that favor." His companions finally prevailed upon him on Clare's behalf, urging him to allow her to come to the Portiuncula and share a meal.[17]

When he was in Assisi he visited Clare often and consoled her. The sources indicate that she needed consoling and that only Francis could provide it. But Francis resisted allowing her to go beyond the cloister. When Clare did go to see him that evening for the dinner, she lingered so long at the Portiuncula that the other sisters at San Damiano grew alarmed, fearing that Francis had sent her to direct another monastery.[18]

Francis was a knight for the Gospel. He answered his call. And his lady answered hers. He renounced everything to embrace his mission, and so did she. He went on with his work carrying the security of her devotion while she stayed behind. She freed him. And he went.

The Sultan

The farthest reach of Francis' life as a mendicant was to Egypt. In 1219 he left the Italian peninsula to join the Fifth Crusade in Damietta, the northern Egyptian port city in the Nile delta. This episode embodies all the drama and improbability that marked his transformation from a knight of arms to a knight of the Gospel. It forged for Francis and for others, by his example, a new paradigm for engaging an enemy in a bloody war that was at its heart religious.[1]

For a period of about two hundred years, between 1095 and 1272, various popes and kings mounted a series of assaults in the East—the Holy Land—to meet ongoing Muslim advancement in the region. These assaults have been called the Crusades. During this two-hundred-year time frame, the Christians mounted eight campaigns.[2] The First

Crusade was launched in 1095 in the attempt to secure the pilgrimage sites in the Holy Land and defend against ongoing Muslim encroachment (this was the only Crusade in which Christians secured Jerusalem). In the Second Crusade (1145 to 1148), Christian forces attempted but failed to regain territory lost to the Muslims. When Jerusalem fell in 1187 at the hands of the powerful Muslim warrior Saladin, the Third Crusade (1187 to 1191) was born. Francis was five years old when Jerusalem fell. He grew up under the shock and sadness felt by all Christendom as it reeled from the loss of these cherished pilgrimage sites. Saladin also launched a jihad against Christians, a challenge answered by Emperor Frederick of Barbarossa. The emperor joined the Third Crusade and met his death during that campaign. The Holy City of Jerusalem was not retaken by the Christians in the Third Crusade, but King Richard I of England, known also as Richard the Lionheart, captured the coastal town of Jaffa and secured some Christian access to Jerusalem. This brings us to the Fourth Crusade, launched by Innocent III in 1198.

Innocent III, the same pope who approved Francis' primitive rule in 1209, undertook the Fourth Crusade at a time when the Church was facing division between its east and west versions (Orthodox and Catholic, respectively). His intention had been to first unite the eastern and western churches under his papacy, and then, as a united front, to recapture the holy sites in Jerusalem. He targeted his efforts on Egypt because it was the primary Muslim power center in the Middle East at the time. Damietta was its main port of entry. But Innocent's Fourth Crusade failed. The Christian Crusaders were waylaid in Constantinople, the capital of Orthodox Christianity. Having been offered generous terms to lend military aid to the son of the deposed Byzantine emperor in return for help in the impending Crusade, the Crusaders agreed, much to Innocent's alarm and against threats of excommunication. The emperor's son therefore got his throne, but then he reneged on the promise to help in the Crusade. Thus, instead of the Crusading army moving on to wage war against the Saracens in the Holy Land, they waged war on Christians in Constantinople. A three-day massacre ensued that, needless to say, embittered east-west Church relations. The knights of the Fourth Crusade never made it to Egypt.

In this emotionally charged context, Innocent III proclaimed the Fifth Crusade in 1215 with the hope of recovering ground that was lost in the Fourth. The pope died a year later, however, and it was left to his successor, Honorius III, to organize and dispatch the next great campaign.

* * * * * * * * * * * *

Francis would not be denied his intention to go, even if it meant death—as all of his companions deemed it would. So in the early summer of 1219, he and a small contingent of brothers said good-bye to their beloved Assisi. Those to whom he bade farewell believed they would not see Francis again in this life.

The group set sail for Syria, where Francis intended to rest. From there they would make the final voyage to Damietta. Arriving in the coastal town of Acre (then in Syria; today in Israel), they were met by the friar overseeing the mission there, an old friend of Francis. This man was destined to become a formidable and controversial figure in the order—the illustrious Brother Elias.

He has been variously described by Francis' biographers as a "shadowy transient figure"; a "grand and mysterious character"; "high-handed, deceitful, self-important"; and a tragedy, according to Chesterton, because "he wore a Franciscan habit without a Franciscan heart, or at any rate with a very un-Franciscan head."[3] In any case, Brother Elias stands out as an example of how a man of improbable disposition can love Francis and likewise be loved by him.

His full name was Elias of Bonbarone, a family name that appears in Assisi's early documents as a noble stock. A legal document dated December 9, 1198, describes Elias of Bonbarone as a "forceful and self-confident" man who once served as first consul of Assisi. Another document in the civic archives leaves the impression that Elias of Bonbarone had been married and fathered a son before joining Francis. A legal record dated 1246 includes the name Guiduccio di Bonbarone as a witness in a legal proceeding—by then the sole bearer of the same family name. Elias entered the Order of Friars Minor probably in or around 1213.[4]

Elias was about the same age as Francis, and they would have known each other as youths. In early adulthood Elias attended university in Bologna, considered among Europe's most outstanding academic centers. Elias himself would gain a reputation as one of Europe's great intellectuals—a contemporary historian describes him as "armed with so much wisdom and so much prudence that he was first among the men of his time, first among the Roman Curia, and much esteemed by the Curia of the Empire."[5] In May 1217 Elias was dispatched by Francis to take charge of the friars' mission in the Holy Land—in Acre, Syria.

Acre was an imposing city adorned with gardens and terraces, Moorish archways, and elaborate fountains. Brother Elias enjoyed the good life there, notwithstanding the contradictions related to the priorities of the order. He lived in elegance and drank fine wines at a bountiful table. He enjoyed social status as a respected scholar and philosopher who understood the Muslims. It is said that by virtue of his command of rhetoric, eloquence of speech, and art of persuasion, he converted several Muslims to Catholicism. His managerial and organizational talents were unmatched.

Francis stayed in Acre only long enough to regain his strength. Then, with his companions—among them Peter of Catanio, Illuminato, and Elias—he set sail for Damietta.

· · · · · · · · · · · · ·

Coming into that bustling port they would have seen ships with banners bearing the colors and crests of an international fleet. The ships had gathered there from France, Germany, Brittany, Spain, Frisia (a small province near Germany), and

Holland, all to answer the call to liberate the Holy Land. Land soldiers and knights had come as well, and their raised colors showed many from the Italian republics of Venice, Genoa, Pisa, Lucca, and Bologna. The colors of the Spoleto valley also would have been represented—colors for which Francis himself had once longed to fight. On the Crusade itself, all of these members of the many nations would bear the same emblem and the same colors on their silks and shields—the cross and shield in crimson on white. Even monks and priests wore them on their habits and mantles.

When Francis arrived at the Crusader camp, the Christian forces had successfully taken a strategic tower in Damietta (August 1218) under the leadership of the king of Jerusalem, the French knight Jean de Brienne[6]—brother of the great fallen knight and Francis' hero, Gautier de Brienne. As a result of Jean's victory—known as the Victory of the Tower— the sultan, Malik al-Kamil, was ready to concede Jerusalem to the Christians. But at the time, the Crusader army was under the command of a papal legate, Cardinal Pelagius, who was described by one historian as a "fanatical Spaniard, fiercely impressed with his own rank." He also possessed "catastrophic theories" about how to win the war, as noted by a biographer.[7] He refused the sultan's terms and demanded that the Muslim leader surrender Egypt along with Jerusalem. The sultan refused. Thus, when Francis entered the camp, the cardinal's forces, having rebuffed the sultan's generous offer, were poised to attack Damietta. Francis grew alarmed.

He grew even more alarmed when he discovered that rather than being cut from the cloth of the likes of the great knight Gautier de Brienne, the Christian Crusaders were little more than a motley assemblage of mercenaries, brigands, and thieves. A notable exception was the French knight and king of Jerusalem who had led the Victory of the Tower, Jean de Brienne. He was described as "large, heavy, tall in stature, robust and strong and so expert in the art of war that he was considered another Charlemagne. When in combat he struck here and there with his bludgeon, the Saracens fled as if they had seen the devil or a lion ready to devour them. In his time there was no knight in the world braver than he."[8]

Distraught at the demeanor of the Christians and dismayed about the ensuing attack of Damietta, Francis approached the Christian leaders "crying out warnings to save them, forbidding war and threatening disaster. But they took truth *as a joke*. They *hardened* their *hearts* and refused to turn back."[9] Cardinal Pelagius rebuffed him. Francis then took his concerns to the second in command, Jean de Brienne. The king of Jerusalem and his captains listened to the lowly friar and "agreed that they should call for a truce with the Saracens and avoid an outpouring of human blood and a great slaughter of men."[10] Nevertheless, all pleas for restraint went unheeded. As history notes, the Christians went to battle with the Saracens in the siege of Damietta on August 29, 1219.

It was the anniversary of the death of John the Baptist, and one contemporary historian wrote, "Saint John must have wanted to have a lot of companions since so many Christians had their heads cut off, as he had been beheaded for God."[11] The Crusaders rushed Damietta but quickly realized they had fallen into a trap. The sultan pretended to flee into the desert, leading the Crusaders to chase him— only to discover the majority of the Muslim army lying in wait to catch the Christians off guard.

A massacre followed. Many Christian warriors deserted. Fortini called it "a weak attempt at resistance." Jean de Brienne and a few others stayed to defend against the Muslim advance. "The battle was irretrievably lost," Fortini continues. "The Saracens had reached the Christians' trench. It if had not been for the great valor of the king, Jean, and of the Hospitallers, Templars, and Alemanni [other orders of knights], all the Christians would have been killed or taken slaves." Five thousand Christians fell and a thousand more were taken prisoner.[12] Bitter and embarrassed after the defeat, the Crusaders buried their dead in the sands of the Nile while continuing to provoke hostilities at the sultan's outpost. So skirmishes continued.

At this point Francis informed Cardinal Pelagius of his intention to cross enemy lines and seek a meeting with the sultan. Knowing it would mean certain death for the ignorant and misguided friar, the cardinal refused to grant permission. Francis respectfully demurred. He left the camp anyway, along with the strapping Brother Illuminato, and headed directly to the camp of the Saracens.

* * * * * * * * * * * *

Sultan Malik al-Kamil was the nephew of the great Saladin, who conquered Jerusalem in 1187. And like his uncle, al-Kamil was numbered among Islam's favored military heroes. He was approximately the same age as Francis and was known as a mystic, a man of culture, and a lover of religious poetry. He studied medicine and surrounded himself with learned men—astronomers, doctors, and Sufis—whom he frequently consulted about immortality and matters of the soul.

In addition to the chroniclers and biographers who highlight this episode, there exists a cryptic reference on the tomb of a counselor to al-Kamil that cites a "visit from the monk," which evidently carried an impact: "The things that befell Malik-al-Kamil owing to the monk (*râhib*) are very well known."[13]

In recounting this episode, Thomas of Celano asks, "Who is equal to the task of telling this story?"[14] It begins when Francis and Illuminato came upon the Saracen camp under a hot sun with a southwest wind rising from the mouth of the Nile. The heat would have been oppressive, and the air would have carried the pall of the swamp. As they approached the city's edge, they were immediately arrested and threatened with decapitation. (The heads of

Christians brought a good price for the Muslim warrior.) The Saracen sentinels, seeing them approach, thought that they may have been messengers from the Christian commander, or perhaps had come to renounce their faith. After seizing them, they led them directly to the sultan.[15]

Francis was received graciously by the sultan, who asked if they wished to become Saracens or otherwise had come with a message from the Christian camp. Francis responded that he did not come to convert to the religion of Mohammed. Conversely, he said he had come to present the sultan's soul to God on behalf of Christ. The sultan fetched his sages to judge whether this man's teaching was genuine.

With the sages assembled, the sultan explained what the clerics had said and why they had come to his court. The sages answered that the sultan was "the sword of the law" and that, as such, he was bound by duty to cut off the clerics' heads. "The law forbids giving a hearing to preachers. And if there should be someone who wishes to preach or speak against our law, the law commands that his head be cut off. It is for this reason that we command you, in the name of God and the law, that you have their heads cut off immediately, as the law demands."[16]

The sultan conceded that he was indeed bound by law to execute Francis and Illuminato. However, he decided to act against his own law, because "it would be an evil reward for me to bestow on [one] who conscientiously risked death in order to save my soul for God."[17] Rather than killing the friars, he set about testing the authenticity of their faith

and Francis' devotion to the cross. He spread before them a
beautiful multicolored carpet decorated with crosses. If,
coming toward him, Francis were to tread on the crosses,
he would insult his Lord. But if Francis refused to walk on
the carpet, the sultan would ask why he disdained to approach him. Francis looked at the carpet—and then walked
in full strides across the length of it to approach the sultan.
The sultan asked why he did not fear to trample on the
crosses. "It is the cross of bad thieves, the symbol of brigands," Francis said. "We possess the true cross."[18]

The sultan was disarmed. Curious now about the scrappy
little friar, al-Kamil invited Francis to remain with him for
an extended period. But Francis declined, saying that he
and Illuminato would prefer to return to the Christian
camp. Telling them he would grant them safe passage back
to their camp, the sultan offered them gold, silver, and silk
garments. Francis refused. He said he considered the sultan's soul to be the most precious possession he could have
returned to God—much more so than vast treasures. He
said it would be helpful, however, if he would give them
something to eat. The sultan gave them more than enough
food and dispatched a military escort to guide them back to
the Christian army.

It is impossible to know the details related to this event.
The scenario described above is a composite sketch based
upon a variety of sources.[19] We do know that Francis did
not die, that Malik al-Kamil released him to come home.
So the implication is that since Francis did not lose his

head, the meeting went well. Francis would have conducted himself there as he conducted himself everywhere,
following the code of knighthood and the command of
love. Some observers would like to have seen a Francis who
viscerally condemned the beliefs of Islam. Others would
have preferred a Francis who acknowledged Islam as equal
to Christianity and Judaism as among the world's primary
belief systems. The reality is, he did neither. Francis set his
own agenda in this encounter and followed it through on
his own terms. Rather than denounce the sultan for his beliefs, he invited him, for the love of God, to become a
Christian, and he was willing to put his life on the line to
prove it true. Love ruled his action. The risk and disgrace
did not matter.

His meeting with the sultan culminates the ideals of
knighthood that Francis brought to all that he undertook
in his life as a religious. As was true of all grand and noble
knights, Francis acknowledged Malik al-Kamil as an equal
in dignity, offering him his life "to save [his] soul for God."
The sultan understood that the friar was offering his life,
just as one knight might be willing to die so that another
knight might live. In the end, this won him, if not a conversion, at least mutual respect and a reciprocity of dignity.

Cardinal Pelagius's ambition during the Crusades
mounted unabated, driving him further inland in an attempt to conquer Egypt. But his attempts failed and he
ended in retreat. In 1229, ten years after the siege of Damietta, Malik al-Kamil conceded Jerusalem to Frederick II.

A thirteenth-century illumination of a meeting between Holy Roman Emperor Frederick II and the sultan Francis met, Malik al-Kamil. In 1229 the sultan made a peace treaty with Frederick and ceded Jerusalem to the Christians.

Francis would not live to see this great event that followed years of bloodshed, but some would speculate that he had had an effect on this outcome.

Jean de Brienne, who served many years as a noble knight, died with honor in 1237 and was buried in Assisi, in the lower basilica of San Francesco, a short distance from Francis' tomb. Jean's sarcophagus is cut from white marble and depicts a sleeping king, wrapped in a robe and wearing an imperial crown. The columns of the bier carry the emblem of the king of Jerusalem and that of the Crusade, a cross and a shield. Inside the crypt lies a knight and king who stood bravely in battle and who, in the midst of war, listened to the words of a friar. Jean de Brienne was buried wearing a brown tunic, as he requested, in honor of the little man he deemed a hero.

Revolt

In the summer of 1220, Francis left the Crusader camp in Damietta and returned to Acre with Elias and the others. Shortly thereafter, a friar named Stefano the Simple arrived from Italy with troubling news from home. Brother Stefano had spent months trying to track Francis down. It seemed that some of the brothers back home presumed Francis dead and had thus taken it upon themselves to change things within the order.[1] The changes involved, among other things, days for fasting and rules about eating meat. There had also been maneuvering about oversight of the Poor Clares. Stefano said that those closest to Francis—people such as Giles and Leo—were being mistreated and shunned. Stefano explained that an all-out revolt was underfoot in

Assisi, and it seemed less a rejection of Francis' ideals than a rejection of Francis himself.

Francis had been sitting at the table preparing to eat with his friend Peter of Catanio when Stefano arrived with the news. Francis looked at Peter, recognizing that they were about to eat meat on a day that according to the revised rules had made it forbidden. Francis said, "Lord Peter, tell me what we ought to do."

Peter said, "We shall do whatever you want to do, because to you alone belongs the privilege of giving orders."

Francis said, "Then we shall obey the Holy Gospels and eat what is put before us."[2]

Soon thereafter he and his companions, along with Brother Elias, left for Italy. This would initiate for Francis a spiral downward into conflict, isolation, and suffering that would carry him to his end.

Returning to Italy after more than a year's absence, he found his order in turmoil. Some of the brothers had instituted revisions of rules about fasting for the brothers and had tried to impose an outside governing apparatus on the Poor Ladies[3]—an arrangement similar to that of Saint Benedict. Benedict's rule allowed for ownership of property and other privileges and protections. This change was an affront to Clare, as well as to Francis when he learned about it, as it violated their unyielding convictions about poverty. Francis learned that under this new policy all satellite convents of the Poor Ladies had been appropriated. The sole exception had been Clare's dominion at San Damiano—a testament to her stubborn tenacity to remain true to Francis' ideals. Francis forcefully reprimanded the overseer who had attempted these changes for the Poor Ladies, but this portended a conflict that would define Clare's struggles throughout the remainder of her life.

The tumult resulted in the inevitable conclusion that the order needed a legitimate governing document—a new rule. The one currently in use had been the primitive rule that Francis had cobbled together in 1209. By 1220, however, the order was numbering more than five thousand friars and needed to be governed by a more cogent document with broader parameters and clearer definitions—and one less dependent on Francis' personal authority. To this end a general chapter convened in May 1220 shortly after Francis' return, during which the order initiated critical decisions. First, it was clear to all, including Francis, that the movement had outgrown Francis' ability to manage it. To help maintain stability under staggering growth, Francis enjoined his friend the bishop of Ostia—named Ugolino—to become the official protector and guardian of the order, the leader to shepherd it through this tenuous time.

Ugolino, who would later become Pope Gregory IX, understood that it served everyone's interest to help Francis and his unwieldy order succeed. It was a popular movement, albeit a disordered one. As guardian, Ugolino was poised to harness the religious fervor Francis had tapped and use it to advance the cause of the Church. For this to happen, however, concessions would have to be made, and

Francis did not easily abide concessions. To expedite the organization Ugolino suggested that Francis appropriate a preexisting rule to govern the order. Francis refused: "I do not want you to mention to me any Rule, whether of Saint Augustine or Saint Bernard or Saint Benedict," he said. "The Lord told me what he wanted: He wanted me to be a new fool in the world. God did not wish to lead us by any way other than this." Ugolino "was shocked" and spoke no more of it.[4] Thus, also during the chapter in May 1220, Francis was given the mandate to fashion a new rule.

Several months later, in September 1220, at the chapter held on the Feast of Saint Michael (September 29), Francis resigned as vicar of the order, citing declining health. He appointed his trusted friend Peter of Catanio as his replacement. "From now on, I am dead to you," he said. "Here you have Brother Peter of Catanio; let us all, you and I, obey him."[5]

It was not a sentimental choice. Peter had been among Francis' earliest companions and had proven true over many difficult years. He had traveled with Francis to the east and was the first to advise him after learning the news of the revolt inside the order. Peter possessed wisdom, clarity of thought, charity of spirit, and humility. He was also trained in law. He was Francis' obvious first choice to ensure continuance of the original mandate and ideals of the Friars Minor. Francis understood that his burgeoning order had arrived at a crossroads and that he was incapable of commanding its next steps. He depended upon the guidance of his good friend at this critical juncture.

With the unwieldy order safely under the direction of Peter and the guardianship of Ugolino, in early 1221 Francis began the process of fashioning an official rule. But trouble loomed. Sometime between early 1221 and 1223 Francis wrote a heart-wrenching "letter to a certain minister," the one leading his order at the time, who seemed to be facing daunting opposition. Francis' letter addressed this minister's concerns about antagonism and possible harm involving mortal sin. It also implied that the minister was considering retreat to a hermitage.

In his letter to the minister, Francis presumed that his new rule would be voted upon and approved at the upcoming Pentecost chapter in May. "May you keep this writing with you until Pentecost so that it may be better observed, when you will be with your brothers," Francis wrote. "With the help of the Lord God, you will take care of these and everything else that is not clear in the Rule." The letter indicates that Francis expected the minister to be present at the chapter with the brothers and to actively participate in the appropriation of the new rule. This demands, then, that the "letter to a certain minister" was written either in early 1221, when Francis was working on the first version of the new rule, or that it was written in 1223, when he is said to have been reworking a second version. If Francis was working on the first version (1221), it means that Peter of Catanio would have been the recipient, since he was serving as minister general of the order at that time. If Francis was working on the second version (1223), Elias would have been minister general of the order, and so its intended recipient.[6]

In the letter, Francis tells the distraught minister to "consider as grace all that impedes you from loving the Lord God and whoever has become an impediment to you, whether brothers or others, even if they lay hands on you." He says, "Love those who do those things to you, and do not wish anything different from them, and do not wish that they be better Christians. Let this be more than a hermitage for you."

Francis also addressed the subject of mortal sin. (Mortal sin is a sin of grave matter, committed with full knowledge and with deliberate consent of the perpetrator.) "During the Chapter of Pentecost, with the help of God and the advice of our brothers, we shall make a chapter such as this from all the chapters of the Rule that treat [the subject] of mortal sin." He then described the guidelines he wished to appropriate in the rule for handling it: "If any one of the brothers, at the instigation of the enemy, shall have sinned mortally, let him be bound by obedience to have recourse to his guardian. Let all the brothers who know that he has sinned not bring shame upon him or slander him; let them instead show great mercy to him and keep the sin of their brother very secret because those who are well do not need a physician, but the sick do."[7]

The implication is that the recipient was contending with antagonisms that fell into the category of mortal sin. Even so, Francis exhorts the minister: "If there is any brother in the world who has sinned however much, after he has looked into your eyes, [let him not] depart without your mercy. If he is not looking for mercy, ask him if he wants mercy. And if he would sin a thousand times before your eyes, love him more than me so that you may draw him to the Lord; and always be merciful with brothers such as these."[8] The minister in Francis' letter seems also to have been considering retiring to a hermitage, prompting Francis to tell him that his advice should be "more than a hermitage for you."

Several factors suggest that Peter of Catanio, not Elias, was the recipient of the letter. First, there is a notable disparity between the recourse for mortal sin as denoted in the letter and as it is described in the version of the rule that was confirmed in 1223.[9] (It is questionable whether Francis himself even wrote the second version, since it eliminates critical Gospel reference that defined his vision for the order.) Second, the comment about the hermitage contradicts Elias's well-known distaste for the hermit lifestyle.

If the letter was written to Peter of Catanio in 1221, it suggests that even under the leadership of this hand-chosen successor, Francis still contended with ongoing revolt and rejection of his vision for the order. The letter suggests not only the nature of the opposition but also the treachery that Francis and his close companions faced as the order grew. It also reveals the way he responded to it. He urged the minister to meet treachery with mercy "even if they lay hands on you."

Francis encouraged the minister to keep the letter with him until Pentecost, at which time he hoped the rule would be approved. Francis assumed that the minister would "take care of these and everything else that is not clear in the Rule."

Peter of Catanio, however, did not live to address this matter at the upcoming chapter in May. He died unexpectedly on March 10, 1221.[10] There is no suggestion in any source as to what caused his shocking and untimely death. The Pentecost chapter proceeded that May as scheduled, and Brother Elias replaced Peter of Catanio as vicar.[11]

The first rule as Francis composed it was rejected. He was then given the task to write a second version. Retreating to a hermitage south of Assisi with Leo and another brother named Bonizio, he began the excruciating process again. As a result, "a great rumor resounded among the brothers throughout all of Italy that Saint Francis was drawing up another rule; thus each alerted another." These dissidents from around Europe gathered in Italy to meet with Elias in his capacity as vicar and to register their dissent from whatever Francis planned to include in the rewritten version—and they handed Elias the task of telling Francis their feelings. Elias did not accept the job. "I have already undergone sharp rebukes," he said, "so if you want, you tell him. Not me."[12]

Ultimately, however, it was left to Elias to complete the unhappy errand. As he approached the hermitage where Francis was staying, Elias shouted, "*Sia lodate lo Signore* [the

Lord be praised]." Francis emerged and asked why Elias had come. Elias responded, "All the ministers of Italy have gathered here because they were told that you wish to draw up another rule and so they say you should make an observable rule, because if it isn't observable they intend not to bind themselves to such a rule."[13]

Francis said he could not and would not change what he had written in the second version, because the words in the rule were the words from the Lord himself. Thus Elias took the second version to submit for approval. Several days passed. Francis grew agitated at not hearing anything, so he left the hermitage and returned to the Portiuncula to inquire about what had become of the revised rule. Elias told him he lost it. Francis would have to write it yet again.

The "later rule" was accepted by Pope Honorius III in 1223. Thus the Friars Minor gained official status as a new order.[14] The rule of 1223 was shorter and more concise than the first version Francis presented in 1221, and contained critical deletions; not the least of these were key passages from the Gospels that had been defining points of Francis' mission.[15]

"Who *are* these people?" Francis said to his few remaining closest friends. (He was referring to these newer dissident members who tended to view Francis as an irrelevant figurehead.) "They have snatched my religious congregation out of my hands. What more do they want?"[16]

Most of Francis' early companions had by this time retreated to hermitages, and Francis himself was driven into isolation with only a small core of devoted friends. Grief-stricken over the loss of his friend Peter of Catanio, as well as the turn his order had taken, he was enduring betrayal, abuse, and scorn at the hands of some of his own brothers. At one point he considered abandoning life as a religious and pursuing marriage, starting a family. At another point he considered withdrawing to embrace the solitude of life as a hermit, "with only angels as companions."

During this difficult time Francis devoted himself to prayer. "Repressing the movements of his nature, he occupied himself with God alone," writes Thomas of Celano. "He often chose solitary places to focus his heart entirely on God. He would spend the night alone praying in abandoned churches and in deserted places where, with the protection of divine grace, he overcame his soul's many fears and anxieties."[17] Bonaventure says, "Francis would make the groves re-echo with his sighs and bedew the ground with his tears."[18] Early biographers stress the great holiness that came out of this time. Indeed, these trials did evoke holiness in Francis—but it was a holiness forged in the crucible of rejection and betrayal amid feelings of failure and depression.

TWELVE

Perfect Love

The words Francis had spoken to Leo along the road about "perfect joy" had certainly been put to the test. His newer brothers were telling him that he was simple and uneducated and that they didn't need him anymore. Yet despite all losses, Francis imposed on himself the disciplines of joy and restraint. He said to Leo during this difficult time, "I would not consider myself a Friar Minor if I were not joyful when they speak disparagingly of me, shamefully reject me, and take away my office."[1] When a brother asked him on another occasion, "Why, if these rebellious brothers displease you, do you tolerate them and do not correct them?" Francis answered, "If I cannot overcome and correct them by preaching and example, I do not want to become an executioner who beats and scourges, like a power of this world."[2]

On one occasion in Greccio on Christmas Eve of 1223, Francis served as a deacon to assist at the mass. Desiring the occasion "to represent as faithfully as possible the lowly poverty of the infancy of the Savior,"[3] he sent for an ox and an ass and brought in hay. Animal smells, for Francis, evoked the true sense of raw grit that defined Jesus' entrance as the Son of God into the human situation.

Otherwise, this was a time of isolation and rejection for Francis—a time when he identified closely with the isolation and rejection associated with the one who had lain amid the cows and hay. Francis spent a great deal of time thinking about the passion of Christ—to the extent that he compiled his own readings from portions of the psalms as part of his daily regimen of prayer.

> God, I have told you of my life;
> you have placed all my tears in your sight.
> All my enemies were plotting evil against me;
> they took counsel together.
> They repaid me evil for good
> and hatred for my love.
> My holy Father, King of heaven and earth, do not leave me,
> for trouble is near and there is no one to help.
> Let my enemies be turned back
> on whatever day I shall call upon you;

for now I know that you are my God.
My friends and my neighbors have drawn near
and have stood against me;
those who were close to me have stayed far away.
You have driven my acquaintances far from me;
they have made me an abomination to them.[4]

At the beginning of 1224, Francis' health began to deteriorate rapidly. "Blessed Francis suffered for a long time from his liver[,] spleen and stomach, right up to the time of his death," writes Leo. "In addition to that, in the course of the voyage to preach to the sultan, he had contracted a serious disease of the eyes."[5] The writers of the legends do not name Francis' illnesses, but they describe their effects. These descriptions have provided sufficient clues to identify in hindsight the multiplicity of ailments that afflicted him.

The problems with his stomach, spleen, and liver, noted by Leo, were the long-term effects of the malaria Francis contracted during his imprisonment in Perugia. Malarial parasites in his blood had invaded and broken down red cells, inducing the bouts of fever that plagued him and that had thwarted several attempts at travel. At this late stage his organs were breaking down. The malarial microbe had enlarged his liver and spleen, and he was experiencing constant abdominal pain and dyspepsia (malfunctioning of the digestive tract).

Leo also mentioned the eyes. During his trip to the Middle East, Francis had contracted a degenerative and extremely painful eye disease called trachoma. His eyes burned and teared, and he could not tolerate the light of the sun by day nor of the fire by night. His eyelids grew thick with infection, and his dabbing and rubbing only worsened the condition. Henri d'Avranches says that Francis' "windows of the soul were shut off by cloud, distressed by a misty veil and unbearable pain."

Leo didn't mention another malady Francis suffered, perhaps because neither he nor Francis himself had been aware of it. In 1978 an examination of Francis' mortal remains revealed that he also suffered from tuberculosis, which had invaded his body systemically and debilitated his general health so much that all other illnesses overruled him.[6] "At length after so much combat, wasted by so many woes, he feels the advance of diverse diseases and knows his spent vigor has lost its resistance."[7]

Francis made two decisions in these last two years that would define his legacy. The first was to retreat to a mountain in Tuscany called La Verna. The second was to return to San Damiano.

● ● ● ● ● ● ● ● ● ● ●

In the Tuscan foothills of the Apennines, the mountain of La Verna was owned by a wealthy landed knight named Count Orlando dei Chiusi. In 1213 the count had heard Francis preach and was inspired to approach him and offer his mountain as a place of retreat. It was "very solitary and wild," he had said, and Francis had gratefully accepted.

The precipice on Mount La Verna where Francis received the marks of Christ, called the stigmata.

Dante described La Verna as *crudo sasso*—a rough crag. The mountain rises from between valleys carved by the Tiber and Arno rivers, reaching heights of approximately five thousand feet (sixteen hundred meters). It is covered with evergreens and giant beeches and oaks, whose roots drive down through jagged ridges. Francis "gaz[ed] at the form of the mountain and marvel[led] at the great chasms and openings in the massive rocks."[8] He spent many hours praying beneath the "*sasso spicco*," a precariously projecting rock, when he wasn't otherwise in the mountain's gorges and caverns. In 1259 Bonaventure himself would have a cell built at La Verna.

In the late summer of 1224, his health declining, Francis rode a mule to this peaceful mountain while Leo walked alongside. Once they reached La Verna, Francis, in keeping with his custom, commenced a forty-day fast intended to culminate on the feast day of Saint Michael (September 29). He consumed only bread and water and the sacrament. He slept in the cleft of a rock and spent many hours praying on the precipice. At times he was so overwhelmed with fear that he couldn't bear to be alone and so would call to Brother Leo: "'The devils, brother, have beaten me severely. I wish you would keep me company because I am afraid to be alone,'" Leo recounts. "Every bone in Francis' body was trembling." Leo "remained close to him all night."[9] Francis prayed and wept often. He spent many hours alone.

One night, when he awoke from praying all night, he found he was unable to move well. He was injured. His wounds required dressing. They involved blood. "His hands and feet seemed to be pierced through the middle by nails, with the heads of the nails appearing on the inner part of his hands and on the upper part of his feet, and their points protruding on opposite sides,"[10] writes Thomas of Celano. Another biographer elucidates, saying Francis "saw in a vision a six-winged seraph, as it were, fastened to a cross with its arms stretched out and feet bound together. And though for a long time he pondered with anxious spirit what this strange sort of vision might portend, he understood nothing about it clearly. Lo, and behold, the prints of nails, as it were, appeared in his hands and feet and his right side was pierced as though by a lance. The palms of his hand and the tops of his feet were swollen."[11]

The phenomenon of manifesting the wounds of Christ is called the stigmata. While the early biographers' testimonies about Francis' life remain inconsistent on many things, their accounts of this singular event remain unified. Thomas, Julien, Henri, Bonaventure, Clare, and others concur that the inexplicable episode that took place on Mount La Verna involved a miraculous imposition of crucifixion-type wounds entering Francis' flesh. Only Leo, who was with him on the mountain, remains guarded about the episode. He says only that "the vision of the seraph filled his soul with consolation and united him closely to God for the remainder of his life."[12]

During a class session I taught examining this incident in Francis' life, one student asked, "Was Francis a Christian?" The ensuing discussion revealed that others in the class were wondering the same thing. Another said, "Francis didn't seem to apply to himself the principles of grace and mercy that marked the way he treated others." Still another felt that "he was obsessed with being like Jesus the way he was obsessed with being a knight. I think he did it to himself."[13]

Some researchers suggest that Francis' wounds were the result of leprosy. Indeed leprosy does manifest itself in skin lesions, bumps, or large raised rashes of varying sizes and shapes, but the notable difference between lesions caused by leprosy and those that afflicted Francis is the matter of pain: lesions from leprosy result in decreased sensation and numbness, while Francis' wounds clearly caused him great pain (according to the witnesses). They also did not involve deterioration of the extremities, another mark of leprosy. Therefore it is unlikely that the wounds that appeared while Francis was on the mountain were attributable to leprosy.

I consulted two medical doctors as to what might account for the stigmata. Both said the notion cannot be dismissed that the body can assume physical manifestations of deep inner longing. They independently cited the medical condition known as pseudocyesis—false pregnancy—when symptoms of pregnancy manifest in women who long to have a child but have been unable to conceive. In these cases, the woman's body takes on hormonal changes and an enlarged uterus, yet without the presence of a fetus. Both doctors concluded that it remains medically possible that Francis' physical body assumed symptoms depicting the inner disposition of his mind. Neither doctor dismissed the possibility of the miraculous.[14]

Whether it was self-mutilation, a skin disease, his frame of mind, or inexplicable divine intervention, those "who were with him" were convinced that Francis experienced a miracle on the mountain. The marks on his body mimicked Christ's wounds, which they believed set him apart with the sign of special favor from God. The event unified an otherwise disparate host of chroniclers.[15]

According to the written legends, at this point Clare seems lost in the shadows. In fact, the opposite was true. Now, as always, she remained a formidable ongoing force in Francis' life. When Francis traveled to the east and tumult erupted in the order, he returned to find that although his movement had betrayed him, Clare had proven more true. Over the years, Francis depended upon her. He solicited her advice when he considered retreating to become a hermit (she said he should not do it), and often sent needy people to her, particularly those who were disturbed of mind. On one occasion Francis visited San Damiano at the behest of the sisters to preach. (He gave a sermon using no words.)

After confronting and overcoming longings for a wife and family, and after having opted not to take refuge in the hermit life, he still faced fears and sadness, failings and losses, and deteriorating health. He needed peace, and he made the decision to go to a place where he could rest. He went to Clare.

By December 1224, two months after he incurred the wounds, Francis said good-bye to the brothers who were with him there on Mount La Verna—Angelo, Illuminato, Silvestro, and Masseo. They remained at the hermitage while only Leo accompanied Francis on the slow descent down the mountain toward home. He yearned to return to Assisi.

But when they reached the Portiuncula in early 1225, they quickly discovered that the same old petty jealousies and quarrels among the brothers persisted—as well as the now-familiar ill treatment of Francis. Francis could not rest. Leo writes, "We who were with him witnessed often with our own eyes frequently how some of the brothers did not provide for his needs or said something that would offend."[16]

In early 1225 Francis decided to retreat to San Damiano. It was extraordinary that he would go to the ladies' quarters, given his strict view of brothers mingling with the sisters. Of the legends and other writings, only two mention this period in its entirety, and both sources are attributed to Leo.[17] Some biographers do not mention Francis' stay at San Damiano at all,[18] and Thomas of Celano, in his *Second Life*, acknowledges only that when Francis "was more worn out than usual because of various serious discomforts from his illnesses . . . it was then that he composed the *Praise of the Creatures*."[19] Even so, no mention is made that the *Praise of the Creatures*—the Canticle, as it is known—was written at San Damiano.

The *Fioretti* says Francis went to San Damiano "to visit [Clare] and console her before he left."[20] The writer adds, "Clare had a little cell made for him of reeds and straw in which he might stay in seclusion and get more rest." He was "very sick and suffering especially from his eyes," and "could not bear the light of the sun during the day or the light of the fire at night. His eyes caused him so much pain that he could neither lie down nor sleep." As he contended with his suffering, he prayed, "Lord, help me in my infirmities so that I may have the strength to bear them patiently."[21]

Perhaps being blind made him more sensitive to the movement of the wind. Perhaps the sweet smell of flowers cleared his head. In any case, surrounded as he was by olive groves, catching breezes off Mount Subasio while resting under the watch of Clare and the tranquility of her garden, Francis wrote a song. It began with the word *Altissimu*.

The Canticle of the Creatures is the earliest literary document written in vernacular Italian, not Latin. Francis composed it with the common people in mind. He wanted them to be able to sing it, for he intended it to be sung. He sang it himself.[22] *Altissimu* in Italian is the way to hurl the word "alto" (high) to its superlative expression. Italians frequently attach the "issimo" suffix to words to elevate their force. And Francis was a true Italian. From the time of his youth, when he tore down fortresses and rallied to arms, to the time he stood naked in the presence of the bishop, to his reach to the leper, and then to his stubborn resolve to meet the sultan in Damietta, Francis threw his heart into every raging fire. At San Damiano, sick and suffering, he called forth one more assertion.

"I wish to compose a new 'praises of the Lord' for his creatures," he said, because "these creatures minister to our needs every day. Without them we could not live." "The human race greatly offends the Creator [since] every day we fail to appreciate so great a blessing by not praising as we should the Creator and dispenser of all these gifts."[23]

Altissimu onnipotente bon signore,
tue so le laude, la gloria e l'onore et onne benedictione.

Most high omnipotent good Lord,
To You all praise, glory, honor and every blessing.

Francis' Canticle expresses an idea later articulated by Dante in the opening strophe of *Paradiso: risplende*—God's "reglowing" or "raying forth" his beauty and presence from the ground up.[24] For Francis, God alone is *Altissimu*—and all creatures have been fashioned to participate in a cosmic performance, one sung in every landscape by each participant in that landscape, and each is unified in the single purpose of giving back to God the beauty and originality of his own personality. For Francis, the Canticle is the score sheet of creation's song. It is intended to be sung with energy. It also takes energy to listen to it—and especially to *hear* it. The song doesn't settle so much as rise. It doesn't dispel as much as assert.

The virtue of humility introduces it. For Francis, sober judgment about one's position before God is the prerequisite for singing the language of thanks: *No mortal lips are worthy to pronounce your name. / All praise be Yours, my Lord, through all that You have made.*

Brother Sun illumines God's presence and is the "*porta significatione*"—doorway to meaning. He is warm and grand, and radiates the life force of God.[25] God is praised through Sister Moon because she is precious and beautiful and clear—*clarite*, Clare's name—the light bearer and reflector of the sun's brilliance. Sister Earth, through gentle assertions, governs all life on the planet, bringing forth fruit and colorful flowers and herbs. God is praised through Brother Wind, who helps the earth, spreading seed and moving waters, and who is sometimes serene and sometimes fierce. God is praised through Sister Water, who nourishes the earth through a force that is unstoppable, cleansing, chaste, and healing. God is praised when peace reigns between neighbors, for to live in peace requires meekness and charity—the mark of humility and true humanity. Even Sister Death praises God, Francis says. No person can escape it. They are blessed who, facing it, have come to find God's "most holy will." Mortality itself renders praise to God because, as a fellow participant in all creation, it offers the chance for human beings to find their place in the performance.

The Canticle is often glossed over as sentimental or reduced to the misguided notion that in it Francis "worshipped" nature.[26] The psalms speak of creation as the Maker's handiwork, making God the agent and creation the recipient. In the Canticle, by contrast, Francis summons creation to give back to God the beauty and originality he bestowed on them. Creation is the agent. God is the recipient. It is not pantheism. It is an exercise in the particulars— sun, moon, wind, fire, points of intersection between this world and the next. God is ever the giver. In the Canticle, earth gives back to God the gifts he himself ascribed to it.

For Francis, the Canticle reflects the vision of God that brings all that exists in this world into harmony. For him it is a song that breaks the knees of the black knight that would slay life's goodness and its hope. To write it, Francis had to place himself where he could hear it—with Clare. Then God came near and rayed his beauty out. Creation raised its voice, and in a small way Eden was restored. Clare and Francis found it there—perfect love—in the upward reach of earth to heaven.

THIRTEEN

Final Assertion

Francis' departure from San Damiano was the last time he and Clare would see each other in this life. In July 1225, at the behest of his friends—among them Elias and Bishop Ugolino—Francis took his leave from Clare. He "consoled her with holy and honey-sweet words and said good-bye to her humbly, as he usually did."[1]

His friends had begged him to go south to Rieti, a place well known for medical care of eye maladies. There they hoped Francis would undergo radical treatment, but he resisted. Bishop Ugolino rebuked Francis, admonishing him "to take care of himself and not to discard what was necessary in his infirmity." Francis then deferred to the bishop. The eye disease had already gotten so bad that the only possible help for

Francis was to find the most skillful advice and undergo the harshest kind of treatment.

He stayed at a retreat known as Fonte Colombo near Rieti. After examining him, Francis' doctor recommended a radical treatment of cauterization—the hope being that he could pull the infection out of the eyes. It involved bellows, an iron rod, and Brother Fire.

"Other doctors opposed this procedure," says Leo, and they "considered the operation inadvisable." On the other hand, Elias, consulted by messenger, strongly encouraged Francis to undergo the treatment, insisting he would help him in any way. Based upon the doctor's advice, Francis agreed to the cauterization—contingent upon the arrival of Brother Elias first.

Many days passed after Francis had sent for him, but Elias did not come. Meanwhile, the doctor visited Francis daily, noting that his condition was growing worse and his pain was intensifying. Days passed, and still Elias did not come. Francis became troubled by the burden this imposed upon the brothers attending him. "My dear brothers," he said, "the Lord will credit you with the good works that you have to neglect in order to take care of me."[2] Ultimately, Francis made the decision to proceed without Elias.

The doctor placed the iron rod into the burning coals as the brothers carefully unbound Francis' eyes. When the rod turned red, the doctor withdrew it from the fire. Francis attempted to look at it but could not tolerate its brightness. He stopped momentarily and made the motion of the cross over it, saying, "Brother Fire, God has made you beautiful, and strong, and useful. Be courteous with me this hour."[3]

The brothers left the room. The treatment, administered without anesthesia, seared the flesh on both sides of Francis' head. "The burn was a long one," Leo said later. "It extended from the ear to the eyebrow." After the procedure, the doctor summoned the brothers back to the room. "My brothers," he said, "I fear to apply so drastic a cautery to the strongest of men, let alone to one so frail and ill. But he did not flinch or betray the least sign of pain. I say to you, brothers, I have seen wonderful things today."[4]

Francis recovered at the home of the bishop of Rieti. There, another doctor examined him and declared that the first doctor had been mistaken—the eye procedure had not only been incorrect, but dangerous. This doctor recommended a follow-up procedure also involving hot irons, this time perforating both ears, as described by Leo in the *Legend of Perugia*: "For years a fluid accumulated night and day in the eyes; and that is why the doctor thought it well to treat the veins from the ear to the eyebrow. Other doctors who were opposed to this procedure considered the operation inadvisable; and this proved to be correct, for it brought him no relief. Another pierced both ears to no avail."[5]

Francis' physical condition, along with the botched treatment of his eyes and ears, caused his distress to worsen exponentially. "His veins [were] opened, plasters put on, and eye-salves applied," wrote Thomas of Celano, "but he made no progress and seemed only to get constantly worse." Thus Francis entered the final stage of his life. The locals in Assisi to this day refer to this time as "his agony."

It was the end of 1225. Winter approached and doctors recommended a change of climate for Francis—away from the wooded mountains surrounding Rieti. Consequently, Francis and his brothers left for the milder climes of Siena, where medical care was among the best. On he went, carried by his brothers, finally settling at a friary outside the city. By early April 1226, Francis' condition had become grave. He was vomiting blood and was in more pain than his brothers fathomed humanly possible. He and they believed he would die imminently. He called for a priest to say mass and administer last rites. It was then and there, in Siena, that Francis dictated his last testament, which Brother Leo wrote down as Francis spoke. It was a final plea to the order to uphold the principles and vision upon which it had been founded:

> Since I cannot speak much because of my weakness and pain, I wish briefly to make my will and purpose clear to all the brothers, those in the present and those to come. As a sign that they remember me, my blessing, and my Testament, I wish them always to love one another. Let them always love and honor our Lady Poverty and remain faithful and obedient to the bishops and clergy of the holy Mother Church.[6]

It was at this time that Elias finally showed up. Francis told him he wanted to be taken back to Assisi so that he could die there, and so the journey home began. With Francis carried on a mat, the brothers stopped first in Cortona, because Francis' abdomen, hands, and feet had swollen and he was not able to tolerate food. When all of them felt he could travel again, they set out once more, passing through Perugia and finally arriving at the Portiuncula in the valley below Assisi.

There, remarkably, Francis revived. He gained new strength and his condition improved. Elias then recommended that he be moved again. Fortini asserts that Elias was acting in accord with the magistrates of Assisi, who feared that the Perugini would attempt to steal Francis' body upon his death.[7] The brothers thus took him to a friary that had been recently built on the slopes of Mount Pennino, east of Mount Subasio, near Nocera in a small town named Bagnara (the region was famous for its healing springs). Francis remained there for a time. But his feet and legs had begun to swell due to his edema, and his condition worsened. Everyone understood that Francis' mortal life approached its end. Because Francis' incapacitation prevented him from wielding influence over how he would live out these final days of his life, Assisi's podestà (mayor), perceiving Francis' powerlessness, intervened and ordered that Francis be brought back to his beloved home. The mayor also commanded that a delegation of the city's knights escort him.

Of the knights who traveled to Bagnara to escort their friend on the slow journey home, many would have known Francis as a youth. Some may have been among his companions who had spent rowdy evenings with Francis as *dominus* when he sang in French and carried the scepter. They would have fought with him in Assisi's civil war of 1198 and in the battle of Collestrada in 1202. Some may even have been imprisoned with him in Perugia. Now, when they gathered in Bagnara, they were at the pinnacle of their knightly careers—after decades of service without the man they knew had always wanted to enter their ranks.

The camp would have smelled of animals, coursers, palfreys, and packhorses. It would have echoed the clatter of weapons and armor being laid aside, sallets and bards, swords and shields. Assisi's colors of blue and red would have snapped in the wind, raised not to ride into war but to carry home their dying friend. Once lean and fleet, that friend was now ravaged by illness. His visage, once fierce and spirited, had drained of life. He no longer smiled with song. His swollen eyes were infected and draining fluids.

It was late summer 1226. The delegation rode slowly down the western spur of Mount Subasio. Stones under foot, the escort trod slowly, stopping when Francis needed to rest and waiting for as long as it took. The grimace of sorrow shadowed all faces. They would have entered Assisi through the gate from which Francis departed many times on adventures. They would have crossed the Piazza del Comune and taken the low road to the residence of the bishop, the same palazzo where townspeople had once seen a young man disrobe before his family and cast his lot with God.

By the end of September 1226 Francis was near death in a chamber in Bishop Guido's residence. With him were his brothers Leo, Angelo, Rufino, Masseo, and Elias, but Francis was weak and hardly able to move or interact with them. Fortini describes, however, one touching moment Leo shared with Francis, joking about, of all things, money. Leo asked, "For how much would you sell the bandages wrapped around your head and this old patched tunic?" Francis smiled and said, "I give you this tunic. It will be yours after my death."[8]

Tending to Francis in these last days was a local doctor named Bongiovanni, who had been a friend of Francis dating back to their childhood.[9] Francis welcomed him, asking, "How does this illness of mine seem to you, Giovanni?"

"*Bene erit*," his friend said. "All goes well."

"Don't be afraid to tell me truthfully," Francis said. "For by God's grace I am not a *cucco* and I am not afraid of dying."[10]

Bongiovanni answered, "According to our medical knowledge it is my belief that you will die at the end of this month or in early October."

Francis responded, "*Bene veniat. Ben venga.* Welcome, Sister Death."[11]

But Francis did not want to die confined behind the guarded gate of the bishop's residence in isolation. He wanted to go home, he said—home to the place where "the Most High gave us increase and illumined our souls and kindled our desires." He was speaking, of course, of the Portiuncula. A canon at the bishop's palace made arrangements for him to be carried to the valley below Assisi.

Once again a procession carrying Francis set out on another leg of his journey home. They went out the gate on Assisi's southern wall and traveled a short stretch along the Strada Francesca, the primary road to France—which Francis himself would have taken many times on business with his father. When the procession came to a crossroads in the valley where, looking back, a commanding view of Assisi dominated Mount Subasio's meandering slope, Francis asked to stop. The group rested near a leper hospital Francis had often frequented. He asked his brothers to turn his face toward Assisi. Though he was so blind he couldn't see his town, he raised his arms and spoke:

Lord, this city was formerly the refuge of the unjust and wicked. But by your abundant goodness you have chosen a time to show this city your riches and your love. It has become the abode of those who know you and who give glory to your name and diffuse the sweet fragrance of a pure life, a solid faith, and good reputation. I beg you, Lord Jesus, Father of mercies, do not look upon our ingratitude, but recall to mind the infinite love you have shown to this city. May it remain the abode and residence of those who will know and

glorify your blessed and glorious name in ages to
come.[12]

. . . .

It is not documented why Clare did not come to him at the
end. She, too, was ill, and, by implication, was unable to
travel even the short distance from San Damiano to the
Portiuncula. Francis dispatched some brothers to take her a
note. "Tell her to banish the sorrow and sadness she feels at
the thought of never seeing me again. Tell her that before
she dies she will see me again and will receive great consolation from me."[13]

He also requested that one of the brothers contact a friend
who lived in Rome, a wealthy woman named Jacopa. She
had been devoted to Francis and had supported the friars fi-
nancially. Francis called her "Brother Jacopa." Her real name
was Giacomina dei Settesoli, a widow and mother who made
special cookies that Francis loved. Francis instructed the
brothers: "Ask her to send some of that grey-colored monastic material for a tunic, like the one the Cistercians manufac-
ture in overseas countries. . . . Ask her to send some of that
cake that she would prepare for me when I was in Rome."[14]

Just as the brothers prepared to depart for Rome, they
heard horses approach and the sound of voices. A large
company had stopped outside the friary. A brother went to
investigate. Opening the door, he saw Brother Jacopa, who
had spontaneously brought cloth for a habit (for burial) and
had prepared the sweet cakes Francis liked. By this point

Brother Giles, too, had returned to the Portiuncula, as had Bernardo, Francis' first follower. Remembering how Bernardo loved Brother Jacopa's sweet cakes, Francis asked his brothers to "give them to Brother Bernardo. The cake will please him."[15]

Francis had told his brothers, "When you see me *in extremis* lay me down naked on the earth and leave me there for as long as it takes to walk a leisurely mile." By early Saturday morning, October 3, 1226, death closed in. Francis' eyes were shut, his teeth clenched, his face in a grimace of pain. The air smelled of damp linens, sweat, and blood. His breathing was labored. Sometimes he moaned. His limbs twitched. Tremors beset him. His fever pitched. He gasped for air. His wasted arms and legs stiffened.

By nightfall, the languor of death descended. Francis asked his brothers to put him on the ground. Angelo and other brothers were singing the Canticle as Francis wept. On the ground he sang his last song, as it seemed creation's voice returned. Francis could hear it, because he himself was singing it and he himself was part of the song. All losses had been righted. All that had been lost was found. His soul folded in on itself and then opened like a flower. Sun. Moon. Earth. Fire. Stars. Evening. Morning. "I call upon you, O Lord. Come quickly to me."

CHAPTER
Fourteen

Those
He Left Behind

"*Before I begin to speak, I sigh*"—those were the words of Brother Elias in the letter announcing Francis' death.[1] Many people sighed that sad day. Francis' death changed everything—not just for the friends and followers he left behind, but also for critical personalities on the social and political landscape of the age. A triumvirate of historical figures—Elias, Pope Gregory IX, and Emperor Frederick II—would intersect in a volatile drama in which Francis was the invisible protagonist behind the improbable plot. Each faced his own drama related in its own way to the impact of Francis. Each played a unique role in the tumultuous events that unfolded after his death, as will be examined in turn.

We begin with Elias. He is at once hailed as the one who ensured the survival of the order and reviled as the one who destroyed it. He is numbered among the most prominent influences in the early history of the Friars Minor—and at the same time is considered the most controversial figure in the history of the movement in the aftermath of Francis' death.

Immediately following Francis' passing, Elias stepped out front and center in the order. Minister general at the time, he dispatched with great feeling the letter announcing the death of their beloved founder. The letter reflects the emotional scope and complexity of the enigmatic Elias:

> My groans gush forth like waters in a flood. Our consoler has gone away from us. He who carried us in his arms like lambs has gone on a journey to a far off country. We would rejoice exceedingly on his account, yet for our own part must we mourn, since in his absence darkness surrounds us and the shadow of death covers us. It is a loss singularly my own, for he has left me in the midst of darkness, surrounded by many anxieties and pressed down by countless afflictions. Mourn with me, brothers, for I am in great sorrow and, with you, in pain. We are orphans without our father and bereaved of the light of our eyes.[2]

In the letter Elias also gives details about Francis' physical appearance before and after death.[3] "No part of his body was without great suffering. By reason of contraction of the sinews, his limbs were stiff, much like those of a dead man. But after his death, his appearance was one of great beauty. His limbs, which had been rigid, became marvelously soft and pliable, so that they would be turned this way and that, like those of a young child."

After announcing his death and verifying the presence of the stigmata, Elias arranged for Francis' temporary burial at San Giorgio, the church where he had attended grade school. Soon thereafter, with Pope Gregory IX (Francis' friend, the former bishop of Ostia, Ugolino), Elias started making plans for the erection of a great basilica in Assisi to be the permanent resting place of Francis' mortal remains. They also proceeded to collect money to pay for it. This predictably alienated those closest to Francis, who doggedly upheld the ideals of poverty espoused by their friend. Francis himself had objected to friars constructing any building for their use, and more so to their handling of money.[4] His closest friends therefore viewed the construction of the basilica a betrayal of his ideals. The "little lamb" Leo is said to have taken a mallet to the marble collection box, an act for which he was soundly whipped and imprisoned by Elias.[5]

The controversy associated with Elias resulted in the decision at the chapter held in May 1227 to dismiss him as minister general and replace him with a friar from Spain named Giovanni Parenti. At the same chapter the then newly elected pope, Gregory IX, initiated the process for Francis' canonization. While that was proceeding, he secured a piece of land at the western extremity of Assisi, the so-called *collis inferni*, or "hill of hell," and construction on the basilica began in March 1228. Francis was canonized in July 1228, at which time Pope Gregory consecrated the foundation stone of the basilica.

The construction work—overseen by Elias, despite his dismissal—advanced with incredible speed. The lower church,[6] where Francis is buried, was finished within twenty-two months. In April 1230 the pope declared the Basilica of Saint Francis property of the Holy See and *Caput et Mater* of the Franciscan Order—that is, the locus of critical documents related to Francis and the order, reliquary, and repository for bequeathals. The following May, in a hurried, secret, and still unexplained change of plan, Elias orchestrated the transference of Francis' body from San Giorgio to the basilica's lower church a few days before this event's scheduled date. Consequently, the minister general and other friars did not have time to assemble. A few months later, after giving an account to the pope as to how such a situation could have occurred, Elias withdrew to a hermitage in Cortona.

In another twist, at the chapter in 1232 Elias was surprisingly reelected to succeed Giovanni Parenti as minister general "more tempestuously than by law," as one contemporary chronicler described it.[7] He governed the order for the next seven years, during which time he oversaw the completion of the upper basilica, which was finished in 1239.

Under Elias, the order prospered. Its members opened themselves to theological studies in all provinces and inhabited *loca conventualia*—larger friaries in urban centers rather than rustic hermitages in the mountains.[8] Elias planted the order in Hungary, Poland, Scandinavia, Ireland, Scotland, and Lithuania, and friars were sent to Morocco, Damascus, Baghdad, and Georgia. Elias also extended the presence of Franciscans among the Saracens in Palestine, North Africa, and in the regions of the Black Sea.

Nevertheless, Elias remains subsumed in mystery and contradictions—in the words of one Franciscan, he is enveloped in a "dark shadow." Elias had been in close contact with then-emperor Frederick II, who in a letter to Elias dated May 17, 1236, acknowledged the holiness of the "Minors" and asked Elias for prayer. At the time, Frederick was alienated from the Church and was an antagonist of Pope Gregory IX. It was Gregory who had sent Elias to Frederick to try to strengthen the relations between the Church and the empire.

Meanwhile, Elias's conduct as minister general provoked the ongoing dissent of "zealot" friars. He refused to convene a chapter during which they would have had the opportunity to air their grievances, and he did not visit any of the provinces. Instead he sent "visitors" who acted as tax collectors to continue solicitation for funds for the basilica and convent. He thus imposed on the brothers the burden of dealing with money. When several of Francis' early and devoted companions resisted, they were called mutineers.

Some were scourged, others exiled or imprisoned. All of this, as one modern Franciscan described it, aggravated the "bad mood" of the time, prompting in 1238 complaints and accusations to the pope against Elias.

Elias attempted to excommunicate the agitators and to prevent the pope's receiving them, but Gregory did receive them. Contrary to Elias's wishes, in 1239 he called a chapter to meet at Rome. After heated discussions and repeated accusations, Brother Elias was discharged from his post by the pope himself. Though he was not excommunicated, the majority of friars no longer accepted him. The friar and priest Alberto of Pisa succeeded him as minister general.

At this point, Frederick II stepped onto the scene on behalf of Elias. Frederick himself had been excommunicated because of ongoing antagonisms with the pope, and after Elias's dismissal from the order, Frederick summoned him to Pisa. Seeing the emperor as a lifeline, Elias openly transferred his allegiance from the Church to the state. In 1240 he rode with the emperor's army on a charge at the siege of Faenza and then Ravenna. Elias later wrote a letter to the pope asking his pardon, but Gregory IX died in 1241 never having received the request. A chapter of the friars convened at Genoa in 1244 and Elias was summoned by then-pope Innocent IV to attend, but he failed to appear. Elias was then officially excommunicated and expelled from the order.

In June 1245 Elias retreated to Cortona and built a church there dedicated to Francis. In the years shortly thereafter, a new minister general, Brother Giovanni of

Parma (1247–1257), sent word to Elias inviting him to come to an upcoming chapter, to make amends, and to reenter the order. Elias feared being imprisoned if he showed up. Moreover, he refused to renounce his ties with Frederick II. The effort at reconciliation failed.

By the time his protector Frederick died in 1250, Elias was a frail old man, alone and isolated. By 1253 he had grown gravely ill. According to the sworn testimony of witnesses, the archpriest of Cortona received Elias's repentance and on Holy Saturday, April 19, 1253, absolved him of all sins. He died on Easter Tuesday, April 22, reconciled with the Church but outside the Order of the Friars Minor. He was buried at Cortona in the church he built, his body dressed in his ashen Franciscan habit. His marker in the floor is now almost indecipherable.

- - - - - - - - - - - -

As for Francis' good friend the bishop of Ostia, Cardinal Ugolino, in the months immediately following Francis' death, he was elected pope, taking the name Gregory IX.[9] Upon his election Pope Gregory promptly ordered Emperor Frederick II to keep a promise he had made to go to the Holy Land on a crusade. Frederick did not immediately fulfill either the promise or the subsequent order, so in September 1227 Gregory suspended the emperor from the Catholic community and threatened him with excommunication.

In the spring of 1228 the Emperor Frederick incited Roman nobles and others to revolt against the pope—they even attacked Saint Peter's Basilica during a celebration of the mass on Easter Tuesday. Some of the pope's own guards had abandoned him, so Gregory IX was forced to flee Rome, retiring first to Rieti, then to Spoleto, and finally to Assisi.

During this volatile and tenuous period Gregory issued the bull *Recolentes*, announcing his intention to build a *specialis ecclesia*—a basilica—in honor of Francis and to house his mortal remains. Three months later, in July, Gregory canonized Francis in Assisi and laid the foundation stone of the new basilica, which he declared to be the property of the pope (since the order itself was prohibited from owning property). He also commissioned Thomas of Celano to write the official biography of Francis. These actions clearly advanced "the cult of the saint," as one writer put it, and early on Gregory employed and empowered Elias to take the lead in propelling it.

We have already seen how in 1230 Elias hastily transferred Francis' remains from San Giorgio to the new basilica, unsettling and alienating the larger community. We have also seen how this and other bold moves on the part of Elias and Gregory changed living patterns among the Friars Minor.

Nevertheless, even among those brothers who wanted to make adaptations to the way of life within the order, there remained a major thorn in the side. This was Francis' *Testament*, his words written near death and addressed to his brothers, whom he feared were losing heart. The document carried the tone of a command, as well as the authority of Francis himself. The resulting factionalism compelled a delegation of friars, including Anthony of Padua, to go to Rome during the spring of 1230 to ask Gregory IX for clarification on the authority of the *Testament*. The following fall the pope issued a bull, *Quo elongati* (September 1230), in which he declared that the *Testament* was nonbinding.

As the Friars Minor was fracturing, Frederick was at Gregory's heels, and heresies were spreading. All of this threatened to undermine the authority and stability of the Church. In 1231 Gregory appointed papal inquisitors in countries throughout Europe to stabilize the situation.[10] Before this, "inquisition" had been the duty of local bishops, so the pope's move seemed to be an aggressive act.[11]

At one point Gregory IX denounced Frederick II as a heretic and summoned a council at Rome to sanction the censure. In response, Frederick II attempted to sink the ships carrying prelates en route to attend the synod and cast their vote. The skirmishes resulted in the death of several representatives from various countries of Europe. Ultimately, Gregory IX himself died in August 1241 before the tumult reached its unfortunate end.

* * * * * * * * * * *

Francis' childhood contemporary Frederick II lived out his career to more gratifying ends. In August 1227, a year after Gregory's election as pope and in response to his command, Frederick II attempted to carry out his promised crusade.

But he was felled by a fever, which derailed his program. So Gregory's command went essentially unheeded. This incident led to Gregory IX's excommunication of Frederick in September 1227, terminating what had been a tenuous peace between them. In March of 1229 the now-excommunicated emperor undertook a crusade anyway. To the astonishment of many, he succeeded in claiming victory when the sultan— the same Malik-al-Kamil whom Francis had visited—ceded Jerusalem to the empire. Frederick crowned himself king of Jerusalem and returned to Italy the following June, and the pope was forced to acknowledge the emperor's success and to release him from excommunication (July 1230). In spite of compromises made by the emperor in deference to the pope's graces, the gesture was a papal concession. It was during this volatile period that the body of Francis was secretly moved from San Giorgio to the newly built basilica.

After Gregory died, Frederick, undeterred, crowned himself *Romanorum imperator semper Augustus; Jerusalem et Siciliæ rex* (Roman emperor in the line of Augustus; king of Sicily and Jerusalem), claiming power over Church and state. He had been setting the stage for this for years. By 1235 he had successfully organized the southern kingdom of Sicily under his rule, and, like his powerful grandfather Frederick of Barbarossa, Frederick had also attempted to reestablish the imperial power in upper Italy in the attempt to restore the *imperium mundi*. He published an energetic manifesto protesting the "empire" of the pope. Thus in March 1239 Gregory excommunicated for a second time the "self-confessed heretic," the "blasphemous beast of the Apocalypse." Frederick continued attempting to conquer the rest of Italy, including the papal states.

According to the "Sentence of Deposition" from the Council of Lyons in June 1245, Frederick committed "four very grave offences." These included "abjuring God"; "wantonly breaking peace between the Church and the Empire"; committing sacrilege by the imprisonment of cardinals, prelates, and clerics; and promoting heresy. It was decreed: "Whoever shall in the future afford him advice, help or goodwill as if he were Emperor or king, shall fall *ipso facto* under the binding force of excommunication."[12]

Frederick responded in 1246 by writing a letter to other kings of Christendom:

Those who are considered clerics, grown fat on the alms of princes, now oppress princes' sons. What is implied by our maltreatment is made plain by the presumption of Pope Innocent IV for, having summoned a council—he has declared to pronounce a sentence of deposition against us who were neither summoned nor proved guilty of any deceit or wickedness, which sentence he could not enact without grievous prejudice to all kings. You and all kings of particular regions have everything to fear from the effrontery of such a prince of priests.[13]

On it went. After an aborted assault on Assisi itself, among other ongoing skirmishes, Frederick grew ill and, wearing the habit of a monk, died peacefully on December 13, 1250, in Castel Fiorentino near Luceria, in Puglia.

And so, in the aftermath of Francis' death—as Frederick threatened the stability of the Church, Gregory orchestrated the "cult of the saint," Elias expedited Gregory's intentions, the Franciscans rejected Elias, Elias turned to Frederick for protection, and Frederick continued to challenge the Church—the poor little man from Assisi who lay dead in his grave was still changing the landscape of his times.

• • • • • • • • • • • •

The lives Francis touched most intimately were indelibly affected, in life, by the force of his personality, and, after his death, by the echo of his beliefs. His first follower, Bernard of Quintavalle, had retreated to a hermitage during Francis' later years and was living in seclusion. The lack of information about Bernard's life after Francis' death implies that the same held true for his later years. He is thought to have traveled to Spain at one point. He died sometime around 1241 and is buried with a few other early followers in the lower basilica of San Francesco, beneath the painter Cimabue's image of the *Madonna Enthroned*.

Brother Giles became known as a ubiquitous traveler, having visited (among other places) Ficarolum, between Mantova and Ferrara; the Holy Land; Ancona; Mount

Gargano, Apulia (the sanctuary of Saint Michael the Archangel); Bari (the sanctuary of Saint Nicholas); and Tunis, North Africa. Known as a seer of God, Giles was sometimes overtaken with ecstasies and "nearly off his balance—but not quite," as one historian described him. He is known to have wept a lot. He approached a priest once asking for alms, and when the priest told him he was an idle good-for-nothing, Giles wept, believing him, because to his way of thinking priests didn't lie. Giles returned to Assisi to be with Francis at his death and thereafter remained especially close to Brother Jacopa, who herself assumed the habit and lived out her days in Assisi. Giles retreated to the hermitage of Monteripido, near Perugia, and died in April 1262.[14] His grave is in the Franciscan church at Perugia.

Brothers Angelo and Rufino are credited for coauthoring (with Leo) the letter that introduces the *Legend of the Three Companions* in 1246. It was addressed to the minister general Crescentius of Iesi, who at the time had solicited written accounts from various brothers of their memories of Francis. They died in 1258 and 1249, respectively.

Leo remained a staunch defender of Francis' ideals after his friend's death and incurred great hardship as a result. When he protested the collection of money for the erection of the basilica—even smashing the marble urn Brother Elias had set up for contributions—Leo was soundly beaten and expelled from Assisi. He then retreated to a hermitage, and hereafter we have only occasional glimpses of him. He appears to have passed his later years at the Portiuncula and spent much of that time writing various works about Francis.[15] Leo remained very close to Clare throughout her life. He visited her frequently and was present, along with Angelo, when she died in 1253. Leo died at the Portiuncula, at an advanced age (his exact age is unknown), on November 15, 1271. He bequeathed to the order three notes written from the hand of Francis, one of which Leo carried on his person until his death. They remain the only extant autographs of Francis and are written in poor Latin. The mortal remains of brothers Leo, Masseo, Angelo, and Rufino are buried around Francis' tomb in the crypt of the Basilica of San Francesco. Leo is placed to Francis' right.[16]

Little is known about what became of Francis' father, Pietro Bernadone. It is assumed that after the incident at the bishop's palace when Francis publicly renounced him, they had no further contact. It is not known if the same can be said of his relationship with his mother, Pica. She was still living when Thomas of Celano wrote his *First Life* and was upset by it, which in part prompted the rewrite.[17] A fifteenth-century source renders a highlight of what became of Francis' brother, Angelo, and his offspring:

His brother Angelo fathered Giovanni and Picardo; Giovanni fathered Siccolo, who fathered Giovanni, Angelo, Petruccio, Bernardo and Francesco, and their sisters Francesca and Chiara. Angelo and Francesco, great grand-nephews of Francis, were Lesser Brothers and lived during the time of Lord Pope John XXII.

Brother Francesco, moreover, lived until the plague [of 1349]. Petruccio fathered a daughter called Francesca who, in the year of the Lord 1365, was still a young girl. Bernardo also had another daughter, Giovanna, who is still alive.[18]

＊＊＊＊＊＊＊＊＊＊＊＊

This brings us to Clare, Francis' "woman of the castle." She outlived Francis by twenty-seven years.

Clare was left to make her own way in a life she hadn't exactly anticipated. She fell ill—so ill, in fact, that she became crippled. For the remaining twenty-seven years of her life she was bedridden and could not walk. She had shown signs of this malady even while Francis was alive, as her illness prevented her from going to be with him when he died. When Francis wrote the Canticle of the Creatures while at San Damiano, he also composed another canticle, this one to Clare and her sisters. He knew Clare wasn't well and that she was going to need ongoing care. The Canticle was a gentle exhortation to the sisters to bear it patiently. He wrote, in part, "Those who are weighed down by sickness, and the others who are wearied because of them, all of you: bear it in peace. For you will sell this fatigue at a very high price."[19]

The exact nature of her illness is unknown, and opinions vary. Her immobility suggests a malady of the bones. Brother Loek Bosch, who lives today at San Damiano, says some think Clare had multiple sclerosis. Another scholar I spoke with believes she might have had rheumatic fever.[20] Many dismiss her malady as a result of her strict fasting, and Sister Anastasia Chiara says there has been recent discussion about it being "a mystical illness."

One historian I interviewed suggested the possibility that she may have contracted tuberculosis, which then entered the bone. Tuberculosis spread rampantly across Europe in the Middle Ages and became its primary epidemic, overtaking leprosy as the more aggressive, faster-killing disease. Tuberculosis of the bone is rare but can be manifested in someone whose body carries the germ, especially if the body's resistance has been broken down. TB enters the bones and joints by way of the bloodstream and attacks primarily the spine and long-bone extremities. A person with bone TB suffers pain, swelling, and stiffness, muscle weakness—that is, true weakness (or "objective weakness" because of damaged motor neurons)—and decreased appetite or anorexia. Unless it is treated quickly, it can result in deformity or crippling. The essential fact, however, is that nobody knows the exact nature of Clare's illness.[21]

But we do know this: sick, cloistered, immobile, and grief-stricken after Francis' death, Clare began the interior work that would define her spirituality.[22] She dug deep inside herself to redefine her sense of God and the purpose of her life. "In the cloister we live as Christ lived in the wilderness, in prayer. It is our desert," said Sister Anastasia Chiara, a present-day Poor Clare.[23] Thomas Merton describes those who live in the desert as having to "swim for one's life into an apparently irrational void; pioneers who struck out into the unknown—themselves."[24] Clare's spiritual landscape after Francis' death can be similarly defined. She made concessions in obedience to Francis.[25] Now Francis was gone and she was crippled. Her desert opened before her unbidden. It was a crucible of testing.

We have noted how Francis ascribed an unprecedented place for women in his movement. Feminine spirituality resonated with the mystical elements of the penitential movement in the Middle Ages, especially as female contemplatives embraced a spirituality called bridal mysticism. Drawn from imagery in the Song of Songs, these mystics experienced their relationship with God as a love affair of the soul in spirit. Clare's outer life deteriorated while her inner life grew more robust as a lover, a damsel, and a bride.

This is evident in four letters Clare wrote to Agnes of Bohemia between the years 1234 and 1253, the year Clare died. At the age of three, Agnes, the daughter of Queen Constance and King Ottokar I of Bohemia, had been betrothed to the duke of Silesia. He died a few years later and, subsequently, a continuous stream of powerful suitors followed. But Agnes, like Clare, had begun to desire the religious life. Also like Clare, in order to claim such a life she had to decline several powerful marriage proposals by various members of the royalty—including King Henry VII of Germany and Henry III of England, and Francis' contemporary the Holy Roman Emperor Frederick II.

Clare wrote Agnes four surviving letters advising her on the religious vocation. She called her a "spouse and mother and sister of the Lord Jesus Christ." These eloquent writings provide an intimate look into Clare's own spiritual evolution. (They also reveal, among other things, that she was a good writer.)

Her first letter hails Agnes as a bride festooned with adornments of her beloved. "He has adorned your breast with precious stones and placed his priceless pearls on your ears." She addresses unmet desire, attesting that there is no shame in yearning. It is positive, she says, since such desire is planted into the human heart by God. True unmet longing, she adds, is a desire for the experience of God. When the bride has reduced herself to poverty, only then is she unconstrained to rise and meet her Holy Groom. He crowns her with precious stones and places "blossoms of springtime on [her] head, a golden crown as a sign of holiness."[26]

Clare's second letter moves from "unmet desire" to amorous symbiosis between the waiting bride and the coming Groom. She exhorts Agnes to see herself as "another Rachel, always seeing your beginning." "The King himself will take you into the heavenly bridal chamber," she writes, and adds that humans are by nature weak but have been made to long for God. So they participate in the process of finding him. They seek. They find. And, finding him, they begin to take on his likeness. The bride bends all purposes to this process of seeking, finding, becoming, and serving her beloved.[27]

The third letter advises Agnes to "look into the mirror" and see in her face the bejeweled spouse of the Divine Husband. As she beholds beauty lavishly bestowed to the bride by the Husband, all longings are answered. "May you totally love him who gave himself totally for your love, whose beauty the sun and the moon admire."[28]

By the time Clare wrote Agnes the fourth letter, she herself was approaching death. This letter was her farewell. Clare anticipated that she would soon "run and not tire" when her Spouse brought her to the wine cellar—"his left hand is under my head and his right hand embracing me happily. . . . [He will] kiss me with the happiest kiss of [his] mouth," she said.[29]

Sometime between 1240 and 1241, Frederick II, aided by the Saracens, assaulted Assisi by first breaching the grounds of San Damiano. The legends say Clare met them and elevated the host, and they turned away. It is probable that her long-standing relationship with her old friend Frederick contributed to his decision to turn back and abandon the attack.

Clare's remaining years carried an additional mandate. She fought with stubborn tenacity for the right to preserve the privilege of poverty for her community at San Damiano. She sought the Church's sanction of it, fought to her death for it, and wanted it in writing from the pope. The notion of cloistered women living in a community dwelling that was not "owned" by an established religious order was alien to the Church, and Clare faced resistance. Yet she defied popes and rebuffed all pressure from anyone who tried to convince her to bend. She wanted a rule.

The "Franciscan bullary" related to Clare's battle for a rule is a scattered and complicated corpus of documents. "It takes a patient spirit of research," one writer said, "to disentangle the complicated early history of the Order in which these documents unfold."[30] Ultimately the bull *Solet Annuere*, dated August 9, 1253, was handed down from Pope Innocent IV to Clare the day before she died. It confirmed the definitive Rule of Saint Clare and granted her and the sisters at San Damiano all privileges of poverty she had fought for. This made Clare the first woman in the history of Christendom to have been granted her own rule.[31]

Her last words as she lay dying, on August 11, 1253, were spoken to herself. "Go securely and in peace, my blessed soul. The One who created and made you holy has always loved you tenderly as a mother her dear child. And you, Lord, are blessed because You have created me."[32]

The document "Notification of Death" was written in distress and haste. It is unpolished with no logical flow and suggests that her sisters were traumatized: "Our Lady Clare, guide, venerable mother and teacher ascended not long ago to the bridal chamber of her heavenly Spouse called by the separating best man of the carnal bond, that is, by destructive death. . . . After earning during this time the rewards of a just payment, one for which she had poured forth the vows of her devotion, turning away from a betrothal with Venus in favor of one with Christ."[33]

Pope Alexander IV delivered the bull confirming her canonization on August 15, 1255. In 1263 Pope Urban IV changed the name of the Order of Poor Ladies to the Order of Saint Clare. Her remains were exhumed first in 1850 and a second time in 1987.[34]

There are more questions than answers when it comes to understanding Clare. The little we know demonstrates clearly that her purpose in life, second only to God, was living for Francis and his legacy.[35]

CHAPTER

Fifteen

Anyone's Saint

A knight in combat fights with the knowledge that either he or his opponent will die. Each looks the other in the eye and acknowledges his foe as equal in dignity and courage. The life of one knight demands the sacrifice of the other. They understand, in an odd way, that the other is giving up his life, or is ready to. The medieval broadsword binds combatants' lives together in a unity of ability, gallantry, and death.

Francis grew up in a culture of violence and sensuality juxtaposed against heroism, chivalry, and a revolutionary view of women. He chose to embrace the latter. He wanted to be a knight like Gautier de Brienne, who rescued the queen. When Francis birthed the "lesser brothers," he envisioned a ragtag fellowship of Knights of the Round Table living a life of chivalry in the hermits' garb of penance.

Little is left of his legacy in Assisi today that would be recognizable to him. After a few subsequent centuries of internal splintering and realignment, by the sixteenth century the three branches of Franciscanism were fully defined and operating in their respective spheres. The sixteenth and seventeenth centuries saw the Franciscans play a critical role in the Counter-Reformation, frequently suffering martyrdom in England, the Netherlands, and Germany. During the nineteenth century their numbers diminished due to effects of the Enlightenment and political upheaval in Spain, Italy, and France. At the same time, the order was flourishing in North America, and varying branches of Franciscans today rank among modern Catholicism's most prolific and influential male orders. The Friars Minor Observants (brown tunic) is the second largest order in the Roman Catholic Church—second only to the Jesuits. The Friars Minor Capuchin (brown tunic, often with long beards) is the fourth largest. All three branches undertake home and foreign missions and have communities throughout the world. The order also includes the Poor Clares, the community of sisters founded by Clare (known as the Second Order), as well as the Third Order (tertiaries) comprised of laypeople, both men and women. (Countless communities of tertiary sisters remain on the forefront of Catholic charitable mission worldwide.) Franciscans have more canonized and beatified saints than members from any other Catholic order.

The image of an unknown woman of royalty, painted by the fourteenth-century master Simone Martini, in the lower basilica of San Francesco, sold in many souvenir shops in Assisi as the image of Clare.

Friars today drive cars, talk on cell phones, access the Internet, and use credit cards. Assisi's shop windows display Francis of Assisi salt and pepper shakers, coffee cups, statues, postcards, calendars, and a multiplicity of colorful depictions and various translations of the Canticle of the Creatures. Images of Clare abound as well. One of the most popular depictions—often in juxtaposition with an image of

Francis—is well known among local historians, friars, and art experts to be that of someone other than Clare. This is, instead, a lovely woman of royalty who became a follower of Francis and was painted by the early fourteenth-century master Simone Martini. One source I consulted speculated she was Francis' friend Jacopone di Settisole. Another written source lists her as possibly being Blessed Agnes of Bohemia.[1] Still others simply deem her unidentified. Yet this image is marketed ubiquitously as the image of Clare. I asked a leading friar why they didn't demand that the image cease being sold as that of Clare. "It is what the people want," he said. This touches upon the contradiction related to the phenomenon of Saint Francis. Sometimes the image is made to conform to the picture of the saint the people want.

Much has changed since a young flamboyant merchant's son prowled Assisi's streets singing loudly and keeping the neighbors up at night. On the other hand, much is still the same. People still make pilgrimages to holy places, and Assisi is now numbered among the most popular. The upper and lower parts of town still hold feasts and competitions under their respective colors during the spring festival of Calendimaggio. Flowers still bloom, and the breeze off Mount Subasio still cools summer nights. The moon still hangs low over Assisi's ancient walls, and the sun still calls forth each new day.

Popes soldier on, as they did in Francis' time, striving to keep the Church strong and steady. The Church generally—both Catholic and Protestant—still manifests the paradoxical combination of being a positive refuge in a damaged world, and at the same time is itself the agent of damage. Religious warfare stubbornly refuses to cease. People still die horrifying deaths under the banner of all brands of religion.

Even as it was summoned in his day, the name of Saint Francis is still appropriated to rally people around troubling issues. Spiritual leaders, social activists, and others identify him with their respective causes, whether it is peace, ecology, or the defense of animals. Francis of Assisi carries universal appeal. He was loved by the common people, and the Church had the good sense to know the institution thus needed him. So those within the context of the Church have likewise appropriated him, though Francis' lifestyle and conviction contradicted in starkest terms the system being modeled by the Roman Church at the time he lived. Everyone knew this. As one friar told me, when Pope Gregory IX commissioned the building of the basilica in Francis' memory, he wanted "a special church for a special man," because the art therein depicts a Francis who "is carrying the Christian world on his shoulders. He is Atlas. Francis is carrying the building on his shoulder while the Pope is sleeping and dreaming. Popes recognized their weakness in front of this man. He is a giant."[2]

Innocent III and Gregory IX were the first of many subsequent popes to see the value in keeping Saint Francis firmly in the hearts of the people. Something about Francis res-

A fresco by Giotto in the upper basilica of San Francesco depicting Pope Innocent III's dream of Francis shouldering the crumbling Lateran palace.

onates with the common man—at the very least some *one* thing about Francis resonates with some *one* thing in someone else. His legacy transcends categories.

In that regard, he would be willing to be anyone's saint as long as those who claim him understand the code he lived by—that of the broadsword. He would be anyone's saint—as long as the appropriation is not confused appropriation. Francis renounced every consolation so that there would be no confusion about his obedience. It wasn't sentimental and it wasn't trivial. He gave up every dream and desire, even noble and natural ones, to experience God in the only way he knew how. He eschewed platitudes that reduced it to a cliché. His vision of God was bound up in all things together. All things, for Francis, were part of his overarching, vibrant, and expansive vision of God. Whether it was his love for nature, his disposition toward animals, his conviction about peace, or his renunciation of wealth, all aspects of Francis' religious life centered on a single core belief— that is, that humanity and all creatures on, in, above, and below the earth are meant to be participants in a cosmic performance presented by the planet in every landscape for the singular purpose of thanking God. And not just thanking God, but thanking him specifically for the one who gave up every worldly dream and desire to stretch his arms on a cross in the shape of a tau. Francis would say those arms make all creatures debtors. The performance is the thank-you. Francis stood on this belief the way he stood on the carpet before the sultan claiming, *We have the true cross.* As he demonstrated with the sultan, it was a stance from which he would not be moved. He would not kill for it, but he would die for it. He would not raise a sword for it, but he would go to the heart of battle for it. He was poor. He feared nothing. The Francis he was, not the Francis many wish him to be, single-handedly demonstrated that the New Testament Gospel of Christ crucified can be lived truly and with integrity in a violent, chaotic, and un-Gospel-like age.

And so our story nears its end. We have stuck our heads into darkened thresholds. We have stepped back through the ages and met a company of players: popes, emperors, friends, fiends, warriors, women, beggars, and bishops. We entered a world of mysticism, chivalry, poetry, and savagery. We found ourselves in an arena of revolution against a backdrop of religious war. We saw people disillusioned and disenfranchised from the Church who were clamoring for God to speak. We saw how Francis stepped up. He lived what he believed and modeled for his world how to live it, too. We saw the chaos he created.

We have awakened a new story. The times are different, but the stage is the same. It is the same predicament—only the company of actors has changed. As was true in Francis' time, so it is today: there are rascals in this story, and there are heroes, maniacs, and saints. As was also true in Francis' time, so it is true in our time: people don't know what to do with this man. Brother Masseo asked, *Why you?* So the question remains—what is it about Francis that compelled popes and others, then and now, to want to claim him? Who can presume to write of these things?

G. K. Chesterton says his biography of Francis was "certain of failure." But he was "not altogether overcome by fear," because Francis, he said, "suffered fools gladly." We who write of him are the company of fools. We sequester ourselves in lonely libraries before unyielding sources and wish courage for ourselves. We are hounded. We tread where angels fear to. Yet, don't you see, that being the fool is the only way to find Francis? That is because he went where fools go. He called himself God's greatest fool.

He gave up every consolation in order to know God. For Francis, the knowledge of God opened in every moment. Every moment exacted a decision. And every decision demanded exertion. Every exertion required strength of a kind he did not possess. Choices had to be made with strength he did not possess toward a destination he did not see. Each moment offered that choice and the chance to exert what it took to execute that choice, even (especially) without certainty of calculable results. Ultimately these little moments accumulated and triggered the transaction. Matter became antimatter. For Francis it involved hard years that culminated in the race to the leper, flesh against flesh. Then it involved a lifetime of staying true. He would say that the transaction doesn't demand the same process for everyone. He would say, however, that it does demand the dismount and the dash to the radical embrace. For Francis, truth of belief comes in the running. Francis would say, *Dismount and run with everything you've got.* Everything may turn upside down at that point. But he would encourage you to make even the slightest decision and then the slightest movement in the direction of that decision. He would say that at that point you will be given another step and then another decision. You will be nudged. That is how he found his way—or, rather, how his way found him.

He saw the whole picture of God's expansive purpose as he lay naked on the ground before he died. Until that moment he had been a traveler on the journey, scratching through wreckage, moment by moment and choice by choice. Francis would say time—this life—renders the opportunity to make decisions. It is the opportunity to find one's part in the cosmic performance of thanks.

Francis was a mystic. He embodied the odd and inexplicable mingling of cosmic and human elements. Many people in our time do not know what to do with mysticism, because it involves mystery. It is easier to reduce it to a statue or to exaggerate it in a hagiography. Francis was a mystic because he understood human nature to its core as it exists in the flesh and in the spirit. That is because he experienced both flesh and spirit, both burning and both thoroughly. And he was not a mystic only, but a mystic who kept his feet on the ground. That is why he insisted that his order be called the Friars Minor, "lesser brothers." Francis understood the human core and, being Francis, he confronted it honestly and unsentimentally. He not only pointed the way to conquer it but also conquered it ahead of those who would follow him, eliminating the excuse that it could not be done.

That, he would say, is what living is for. It involves loneliness, at times hopelessness. Francis would say it involves shame. Even amid chaos and wreckage you begin to believe you will find what you are looking for, or that it will find you, even if the only thing you see for a time is the wreck.

It commands strength you do not possess. It involves looking for something you can't quite see. Francis says, *Take heart!* There will never be enough certainty in this life to convince anyone of the truth of a fool. The story of Francis of Assisi is the story of a man who went where fools go. It is a canticle. It is waiting while not seeing, hoping and acting in hope as if the promise were as clear as a new day. He sang his song in gentle airs. It came to him in the final moments of his life, naked on the ground, when he hurled it into light.

Acknowledgments

I am indebted to the following individuals, who helped me immeasurably in this undertaking: my editor at Basic Books, Lara Heimert, who eagerly assisted and guided me throughout this project; my agent, Giles Anderson, who got it in the hands of the right publisher; and especially to James Morgan, whose meticulous eye and good sense greatly elevated this book. I am also grateful to the students of Gordon College, to whom I taught courses on Francis of Assisi and whose enthusiasm and inquiry strengthened this book. They are (Wenham, Massachusetts): Devon Abts, Garrett and Liz Brown, Mary Buchanan, Amy Carboneau, Katie Ernst, Rob Gifford, Auri Halsey, Jenny Harris, Peter Mark Ingalls, Kim Kurczy, Jenna Nordberg, Matt Plumb, Luke Retterath, Katie Rice, and Lora Traffie; and (Orvieto, Italy) Michele Calandra, Susanna Carey, Jean-Claire Cheveallier, Jenni Damiani, Lauren Hartle, Sarah Hartlett, Hannah McBride, Sarah Neel, Alli Petrone, Dellynne Strawbridge, and Andrew Wardwell. I thank my son Jonathan Zoba, who designed the maps and, awaking one morning during a visit to Assisi, gave me the title for this book.

I also owe a debt of gratitude to many friars, sisters, Catholic overseers, and other experts who generously gave their time and engaged my questions. I am profoundly grateful to Assisi's bishop, Monsignore Domenico Sorrentino, who received me warmly on numerous occasions. Tour guide and historian Simona Fanelli aided me greatly. And for their help I am grateful to Brother Carlo Bottero, O.F.M. Conv., chief librarian at the Biblioteca Sacro Convento; Sister Chiara Anastasia (Poor Clares); Brother Loek Bosch, O.F.M. Obs.; Sister Clotilde Mizzi of the Franciscan Missionaries of the Immaculate Heart of Mary (Egypt); P. Pier Damiano Lanuti, O.F.M. Obs.; Ettore Bassi; Valentina DiMaggio; Gerard Pieter Freeman; Chiara Frugoni; Alessandro Lardani; Alberto Romano; and Angela Maria Seracchioli. To one whose footprints are all over this book I say an affectionate *Quod es, hoc es!*

Finally, I gratefully acknowledge those rare individuals in whose judgment I entrusted feedback on early drafts. I owe deep thanks to professor John Skillen, of Orvieto, Italy, and to a certain Franciscan brother and fellow pilgrim (he knows who he is) in Assisi. Both of these friends rendered generous input on needed improvements with scrutiny, goodwill, and humor. I extend to them a special *pace e bene.*

Appendix A:
Maps

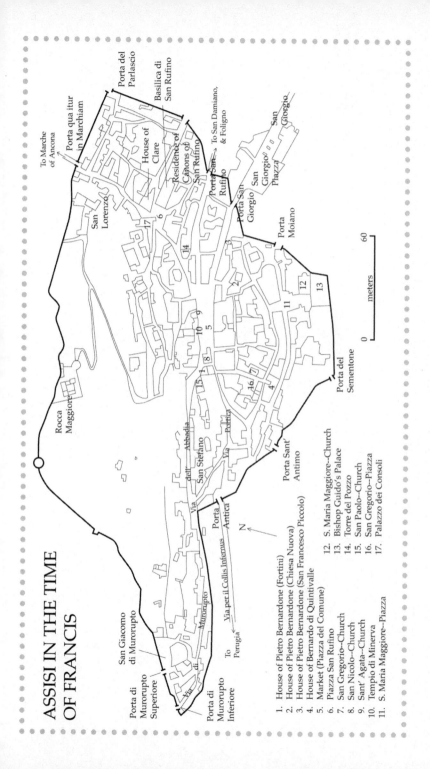

ASSISI IN THE TIME OF FRANCIS

To Marche of Ancona

Porta qua itur in Marchiam

Porta del Parlascio

Basilica di San Rufino

House of Clare

Residence of Canons of San Rufino

To San Damiano, & Foligno

San Lorenzo

Porta San Rufino

San Giorgio Piazza

San Giorgio

Porta Moiano

Porta del Sementone

Rocca Maggiore

dell'Abbadia

San Stefano

Via Paolta

Porta Sant' Antimo

Porta Antica

Via per il Collis Infernus

To Perugia

Via di Murorupto

San Giacomo di Murorupto

Porta di Murorupto Superiore

Porta di Murorupto Inferiore

N

meters

0   60

1. House of Pietro Bernardone (Fortini)
2. House of Pietro Bernardone (Chiesa Nuova)
3. House of Pietro Bernardone (San Francesco Piccolo)
4. House of Bernardo di Quintivalle
5. Market (Piazza del Comune)
6. Piazza San Rufino
7. San Gregorio–Church
8. San Nicolo–Church
9. Sant' Agata–Church
10. Tempio di Minerva
11. S. Maria Maggiore–Piazza
12. S. Maria Maggiore–Church
13. Bishop Guido's Palace
14. Torre del Pozzo
15. San Paolo–Church
16. San Gregorio–Piazza
17. Palazzo dei Consoli

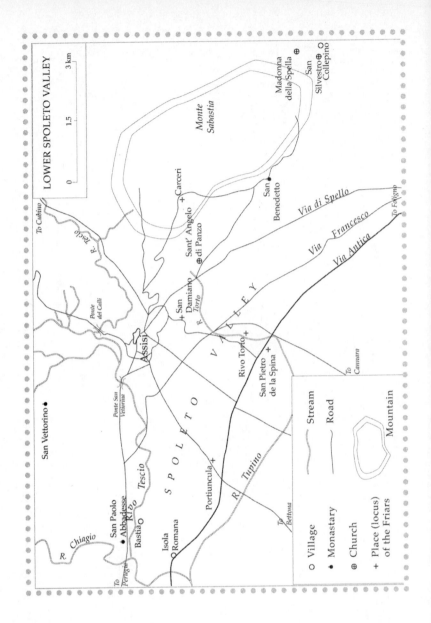

LOWER SPOLETO VALLEY

0   1.5   3 km

To Cubbio

R. Tescio

Ponte del Calli

San Vettorino

Ponte San Vettorina

Assisi

Rio Tescio

SPOLETO VALLEY

San Paolo
Abbadesse
Bastia
Isola Romana
R. Chiagio
To Perugia

Portiuncula

R. Tupino

To Bettona

+ San Damiano
R. Torto
Sant' Angelo
⊕ di Panzo

Rivo Torto +

San Pietro
de la Spina +

To Cannara

+ Carceri

Monte Sabastia

Madonna
della Spella ⊕

San
Silvestro ⊕ ○
Collepino

San
Benedetto •

Via di Spello

Via Francesco

Via Antica

To Foligno

○ Village
• Monastary
⊕ Church
+ Place (locus)
   of the Friars

~~~ Stream
—— Road
⬭ Mountain

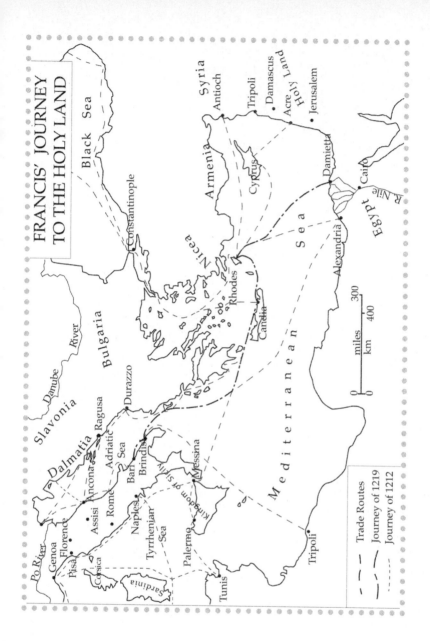

FRANCIS' JOURNEY
TO THE HOLY LAND

Black Sea

Syria
Antioch
Tripoli
Damascus
Acre
Holy Land
Jerusalem

Constantinople

Armenia

Nicaea

Cyprus

Damietta

Rhodes

Egypt
Cairo
R. Nile

Alexandria

Candia

Mediterranean Sea

Bulgaria

Danube River

Slavonia

Dalmatia
Ragusa

Durazzo

Adriatic Sea
Ancona
Bari
Brindisi

Assisi
Rome

Messina
Kingdom of Sicily

Naples
Palermo

Po River
Genoa
Florence
Pisa

Corsica

Tyrrhenian Sea

Sardinia

Tunis

Tripoli

miles 300
km 400
0

Trade Routes
Journey of 1219
Journey of 1212

ITALIAN PENINSULA
POLITICAL REGIONS, 1220

0   50   100 miles
0   50 100 km

Lugano
Milano
Pavia
Alessandria
Genoa
Parma
Modena
HOLY ROMAN EMPIRE
Venice
Ravenna
Rimini
Fano
PAPAL STATES
Lucca
Florence
Pisa
Ancona
Perugia
Assisi
PETER'S PATRIMONY
Rome

Adriatic
Sea

Foggia
Benevento
Venosa
Bari
Naples
KINGDOM OF SICILY
(APULIA)
Salerno
Potenza
Brindisi

Tyrrhenian
Sea

Ionian
Sea

Palermo
Messina
Trapani
KINGDOM
OF
SICILY
Catania
Syracuse

Mediterranean   Sea

Appendix B:
Source Material

* * * * * * * * * * * *

The following source material, with the exception of the author's English translation of *The Canticle*, was taken from www.franciscan-archive.org.

THE CANTICLE OF THE CREATURES

CANTICUM FRATRIS SOLIS LAUDES CREATURARUM

Altissimu onnipotente bon signore,
tue so le laude, la gloria e l'onore et onne benedictione.

Ad te solo, altissimo, se konfano,
et nullu homo ene dignu te mentovare.
Laudato sie, mi signore, cun tucte le tue creature,
spetialmente messor lo frate sole,
lo qual'è iorno, et allumini noi per loi.
Et ellu è bellu e radiante cun grande splendore,
de te, altissimo, porta significatione.
Laudato si, mi signore, per sora luna e le stelle,
in celu l'ài formate clarite et pretiose et belle.
Laudato si, mi signore, per frate vento,
et per aere et nubilo et sereno et onne tempo,
per lo quale a le tue creature dai sustentamento.
Laudato si, mi signore, per sor aqua,
la quale è multo utile et humile et pretiosa et casta.
Laudato si, mi signore, per frate focu,

per lo quale enn' allumini la nocte,
ed ello è bello et iocundo et robustoso et forte.
Laudato si, mi signore, per sora nostra matre terra,
la quale ne sustenta et governa,
et produce diversi fructi con coloriti flori et herba.
Laudato si, mi signore, per quelli ke perdonano per lo tuo amore,
et sostengo infirmitate et tribulatione.
Beati quelli ke 'l sosterrano in pace,
ka da te, altissimo, sirano incoronati.
Laudato si, mi signore, per sora nostra morte corporale,
da la quale nullu homo vivente pò skappare.
Guai acquelli, ke morrano ne le peccata mortali:
beati quelli ke trovarà ne le tue sanctissime voluntati,
ka la morte secunda nol farrà male.
Laudate et benedicete mi signore,
et rengratiate et serviateli cun grande humilitate.
The Canticle (English Translation)

Most High, All-powerful, All-good, Lord!
All praise is Yours, all glory, all honor
And all blessing.
To You alone, Most High, do they belong.
No mortal lips are worthy
to pronounce your name.
All praise be Yours, my Lord, through all that You have made,
And first my lord Brother Sun,
who brings the day; and light you give to us through him.
How beautiful is he, how radiant in his splendor!
Of You, Most High, he is the portal of meaning.
All praise is Yours, my Lord, through Sister Moon and Stars;
In the heavens You have made them, bright
and precious and fair.
All praise is Yours, my Lord, through Brothers Wind and Air,
and fair and stormy, all the weather's moods,
by which You cherish all that You have made.
All praise is Yours, my Lord, through Sister Water,
So useful, lowly, precious, and pure.
All praise is Yours, my Lord, through Brother Fire,
Through whom You brighten up the night.
How beautiful he is, how playful!
Full of power and strength.

All praise is Yours, my Lord, through Sister Earth, our mother,
Who feeds us in her sovereignty and produces
various fruits and colored flowers and herbs.
All praise is Yours, my Lord,
through those who grant pardon for love of You;
through those who endure sickness and trial.
They are blessed who endure in peace,
By You, Most High,
they will be crowned.
All praise is Yours, my Lord,
through Sister Bodily Death, from whose embrace
no mortal can escape.
Woe to those who die in mortal sin,
They are blessed whom you find doing Your holy will!
The second death can do no harm to them.
Praise and bless my Lord,
and give Him thanks,
and serve Him with great humility.

BULL OF CANONIZATION, FRANCIS

Pope Gregory IX
Bishop Servant of the Servants of God *for an everlasting memorial*
July 16, 1228 A.D.

1. How wondrously considerate of us is God's pity! How priceless a love of charity which would sacrifice a Son to redeem a slave! God neither neglected the gifts of His mercy nor failed to protect uninterruptedly the vineyard planted by His hand. He sent laborers into it at the eleventh hour to cultivate it, and with their hoes and plowshares to uproot the thorns and thistles, as did Samgar when he killed 600 Philistines (Judges 3:31). After the copious branches were pruned and the sucker roots with the briars were pulled out, this vineyard will produce a luscious, appetizing fruit, one capable of storage in the wine cellar of eternity, once purified in the wine-press of patience. Wickedness had indeed blazed like fire, and the human heart had grown cold, so as to destroy the wall surrounding this vineyard, just as the attacking Philistines were destroyed by the poison of worldly pleasures.

2. Behold how the Lord, when He destroyed the earth by water, saved the just man with a contemptible piece of wood (Wis. 10:4), did not allow the scepter of

the ungodly to fall upon the lot of the just (Ps. 124:3). Now, at the eleventh hour, he has called forth his servant, Blessed Francis, a man after His own heart (I Sam. 13:14). This man was a light, despised by the rich, nonetheless prepared for the appointed moment. Him the Lord sent into his vineyard to uproot the thorns and thistles. God cast down this lamp before the attacking Philistines, thus illumining his own land and with earnest exhortation warning it to be reconciled with God.

3. On hearing within his soul his Friend's voice of invitation Francis without hesitation arose, and as another Samson strengthened by God's grace, shattered the fetters of a flattering world. Filled with the zeal of the Spirit and seizing the jawbone of an ass, he conquered not only a thousand, but many thousands of Philistines (Judges 15:15–16) by his simple preaching, unadorned with the persuasive words of human wisdom (I Cor. 1:17), and made forceful by the power of God, who chooses the weak of this world to confound the strong (I Cor. 1:17). With the help of God he accomplished this: God who touches mountains and they smoke (Ps. 103:32), so bringing to spiritual service those who were once slaves to the allurements of the flesh. For those who died to sin and live only for God and not for themselves (namely, whose worse part has died), there flowed from this jawbone an abundant stream of water: refreshing, cleansing, rendering fruitful the fallen, downtrodden and thirsty. This river of water reaching unto eternal life (John 7:38), could be purchased without silver and without cost (Is. 55:1), and like branches far and wide its rivulets watered the vineyard, whose branches extended unto the sea and its boughs unto the river (Ps. 79:12).

4. After the example of our father Abraham, this man forgot not only his country and acquaintances, but also his father's house, to go to a land which the Lord had shown him by divine inspiration (Gen. 12). Pushing aside any obstacle he pressed on to win the prize of his heavenly call (Phil. 3:14). Conforming himself to Him (Rom. 8:29) who, though rich, for our sake became poor (II Cor. 8:9), he unburdened himself of a heavy load of material possessions so as to pass easily through the narrow gate (Matt. 7:13). He distributed his wealth to the poor, so that his justice might endure forever (Ps. 111:9).

5. Nearing the land of vision he offered his own body as a holocaust to the Lord upon one of the mountains indicated to him (Gen 22:2), the mountain which is the excellence of faith. His flesh, which now and then had tricked him, he sacrificed as Jephte his only daughter (Judges 11:34), lighting under it the fire of love, punishing it with hunger, thirst, cold, nakedness and with many fasts and vigils. When it had been crucified with its vices and concupiscences (Gal. 5:24), he could say with the Apostle: *"I live now, not I, but Christ lives in me"* (Gal. 2:20). For he really did not live for himself any longer, but rather for Christ, who died for our sins and rose for our justification (Rom. 4:25), that we might no longer be slaves to sin (Rom. 6:6).

6. Uprooting his vices and like Jacob arising at the Lord's command (Gen. 35:1–11) he renounced wife and farm and oxen and all which might distract those invited to the great feast (Luke 14:15–20), and took up the battle with the world, the flesh and the spiritual forces of wickedness on high. And as he had received the sevenfold grace of the Spirit and the help of the eight beatitudes of the Gospel, he journeyed to Bethel, the house of God, on a path which he had traced in the fifteen steps of the virtues mystically represented in the psalter (gradual psalms). After he had made of his heart an altar for the Lord, he offered upon it the incense of devout prayers to be taken up to the Lord at the hands of angels whose company he would soon join.

7. But that he might not be the only one to enjoy the blessings of the mountain, clinging exclusively to the embraces of Rachel, as it were to a life of contemplation lovely but sterile, he descended to the forbidden house of Leah to lead into the desert the flock fertile with twins (Cant. 4:2) and seeking pastures of life (Gen. 29). There, where the manna of heavenly sweetness restores all who have been separated from the noisy world, he would be seated with the princes of his people and crowned with the crown of justice. Sowing his seed in tears, he would come back rejoicing carrying his sheaves to the storehouse of eternity (Ps. 125:5–6).

8. Surely he sought not his own interests (Phil. 2:21), but those of Christ, serving Him zealously like the proverbial bee. As the morning star in the midst of a cloud, and as the moon at the full (Eccles. 50:6), he took in his hands a lamp with which to draw the humble by the example of his glorious deeds, and a trumpet wherewith to recall the shameless with stern and fearsome warnings from their wicked abandon. Thus strengthened by charity he courageously took possession of the Midianite camp (Judges 7:16–22), that is, the camp of those who contemptuously disregard the teaching of the Church, with the support of Him who encompassed the whole world by His authority, even while still cloistered in the Virgin's womb. He captured the weapons on which the well-armed man trusted while guarding his house and parceling out his spoils (Luke 11:21–22), and he led captivity captive in submission to Jesus Christ (Eph. 4:8).

9. After defeating the threefold earthly enemy, he did violence to the Kingdom of Heaven and seized it by force (Matt. 11:12). After many glorious battles in this life he triumphed over the world, and he who was knowingly unlettered and wisely foolish, happily returned to the Lord to take the first place before many others more learned.

10. Plainly a life such as his, so holy, so passionate, so brilliant, was enough to win him a place in the Church Triumphant. Yet, because the Church Mili-

tant, which can only observe the outer appearances, does not presume to judge on its own authority those not sharing its actual state, it proposes for veneration as Saints only those whose lives on earth merited such, especially because an angel of Satan sometimes transforms himself into an angel of light (II Cor. 11:14). In his generosity the omnipotent and merciful God has provided that the aforementioned Servant of Christ did come and serve Him worthily and commendably. Not permitting so great a light to remain hidden under a bushel, but wishing to put it on a lampstand to console those dwelling in the house of light (Matt. 5:15), God declared through many brilliant miracles that his life has been acceptable to God and his memory should be honored by the Church Militant.

11. Therefore, since the wondrous events of his glorious life are quite well known to Us because of the great familiarity he had with Us while we still occupied a lower rank, and since We are fully convinced by reliable witnesses of the many brilliant miracles, We and the flock entrusted to Us, by the mercy of God, are confident of being assisted at his intercession and of having in Heaven a patron whose friendship We enjoyed on earth. With the consultation and approval of our Brothers [i.e., the cardinals], We have decreed that he be enrolled in the catalogue of saints worthy of veneration.

12. We decree that his birth be celebrated worthily and solemnly by the universal Church on the fourth of October, the day on which he entered the Kingdom of heaven, freed from the prison of the flesh.

13. Hence, in the Lord We beg, admonish and exhort all of you, We command you by this apostolic letter, that on this day reserved to honor his memory, you dedicate yourselves more intensely to the divine praises, and humbly to implore his patronage, so that through his intercession and merits you might be found worthy of joining his company with the help of Him who is blessed forever. Amen.

Given at Perugia, on the fourteenth Kalends of August, in the second year of Our pontificate.

MODERN STATISTICS OF THE
THREE PRIMARY ORDERS OF FRIARS MINOR

OFM Observant: The Observants comprise 1,500 houses in about 100 provinces with about 16,000 members. This order is now called simply the Order of Friars Minor.

OFM Conventual: The Conventuals consist of 290 houses worldwide with almost 5,000 friars in the world. They are located in Italy, the United States, Canada, Australia, and throughout South/Central America, and Africa.

OFM Capuchin: The Capuchin Franciscans are the youngest branch of Franciscans, going back to 1525, when some Friars Minor in eastern Italy wanted to live a stricter life of prayer and poverty closer to the original intentions of Francis. The new branch received early recognition and grew fast, first in Italy, and then throughout the rest of Europe. The name Capuchins refers to the peculiar shape of the long hood; originally a nickname, it has assumed the official name of the order. Capuchins exist in 99 countries all over the world, with approximately 11,000 brothers living in more than 1,800 communities (fraternities, friaries).

LIST OF POPES AND MINISTERS GENERAL
FOR THE FRIARS MINOR

FROM THE TIME OF FRANCIS
TO THE FOURTEENTH CENTURY

POPES

Innocent III	1198–1216
Honorius III	1216–1227
Gregory IX	1227–1241
Celestine IV	1241
Innocent IV	1243–1254
Alexander IV	1254–1261
Urban IV	1262–1264
Clement IV	1265–1268
Blessed Gregory X	1271–1276
Blessed Innocent V	1276
Adrian V	1276
John XXI	1276–1277
Nicholas III	1272–1280
Martin IV	1281–1285
Honorius IV	1285–1287
Nicholas IV	1288–1292
Celestine V	1294
Boniface VIII	1294–1303
Blessed Benedict XI	1303–1304
Clement V	1305–1314
John XXII	1316–1334

MINISTERS GENERAL, FRIARS MINOR

Francis of Assisi	1209–1220
Vicar Peter Catanii	1220–1221
Vicar Elias	1221–1227
Vicar John Parenti	1227–1232
Vicar Elias Bonbarone	1232–1239
Albert of Pisa	1239–1240
Haymo of Faversham	1240–1243
Crescentius of Iesi	1244–1247
Giovanni of Parma	1247–1257
Saint Bonaventure	1257–1274
Girolam Masci d'Ascoli	1274–1279
Bonagratia of Bologna	1279–1285
Arlotto of Prato	1285–1287
Matteo de Acquasparta	1287–1289
Raimund Godefroy	1289–1295
Giovanni Mincio of Murrovalle	1296–1304
Gonsalvus Hispanus	1304–1313
Alessando Bonini di Alessandria	1313–1314
Michael of Cesana	1316–1328

Notes

• • • • • • • • • • • • •

PREFACE

1. G. K. Chesterton, *Saint Francis of* Assisi (Garden City, NY: Doubleday/ Image, 1989), 103–104.

2. G. K. Chesterton, *Orthodoxy* (Westport, CT: Greenwood Press, 1974), 169.

3. The citation comes from *Legend of Perugia*, in St. *Francis of Assisi Writings and Early Biographies, English Omnibus of the Sources for the Life of St. Francis* (hereafter cited as *Omnibus*), ed. Marion A. Habig; trans. Raphael Brown, Benen Fahy, Placid Hermann, Paul Oligny, Nest de Robeck, Leo Sherley-Price (Quincy, IL: Franciscan Press, 1991), 1080. It is also found in Bonaventure's *Major Life*, VI:3. The particular translation noted above comes from Julien Green, *God's Fool*, trans. Peter Heinegg (San Francisco: Harper & Row, 1985), 194.

As noted, source material for the early documents relating to Saint Francis is replete with great textual difficulties. The early biography known as the *Legend of Perugia* is thought to be a compilation of remembrances from the pen of Francis' close friend and emanuensis Brother Leo. A fourteenth-century friar, Ubertino da Casale, notes in a document dated 1305 that certain scrolls (*rotuli*) known to have come from the hand of Brother Leo had been lost. Later he refers again to Brother Leo's scrolls, which he claimed to have had before him, suggesting they had been found. The textual history of the document referred to as the *Legend of Perugia* is beyond the purview of this examination. Plenty can be read about it in the sources provided in the bibliography. The writer attributes passages cited from the *Legend of Perugia* as having come from the pen of Brother Leo. All references from this source are found in the *Omnibus*.

4. Details denoting the hasty canonization process are delineated in Jacques Dalarun, *The Misadventure of Francis of Assisi: Toward a Historical Use of the*

Franciscan Legends, trans. Edward Hagman (St. Bonaventure, NY: Franciscan Institute Publications, 2002), 124 ff.

5. Clare's important role in Francis' life is acknowledged by all of his biographers. However, the scope and depth of the relationship is absent from their official biographies. Clare is honored in her own right in a separate legend attributed to Thomas of Celano. But their lives, as denoted in the official written record, were tracked separately.

6. Paschal Robinson, "St. Clare," in *Franciscan Essays,* ed. Paul Sabatier et al. (Aberdeen: University Press, 1912), 31–49.

7. Bonaventure would serve for sixteen years, the longest term of any minister general.

8. For a comprehensive listing of these writings, see Jacques Dalarun, *Misadventure,* 25.

9. These include *Fasciculus chronicarum ordinis minorum* by Mariano of Florence (Observant, early fifteenth century); *Cronicas da orden dos frades menores* (1557) by Mark of Lisbon (in Portuguese); the *Historiae seraphicae religionis libri tres* by Pietro Ridolfi of Tossignano (Conventual, 1586) and *De origene seraphicae religionis franciscane* (1587) by Francesco Gonzaga (Observant). Most notable is the *Annales minorum* by Luke Wadding (1625). Jacques Dalarun asserts Wadding's contribution is "the first attempt to use the legends in a truly critical way." *Misadventure,* 27. For an in-depth discussion of these sources see Dalarun, *Misadventure,* 26–29.

10. Dalarun, *Misadventure,* 21.

11. Paul Sabatier, *Vie de S. François d'Assise* (Paris, 1894 and 1931). Italian trans. C. Ghidaglia and C. Pontani, *Vita di San Francesco d'Assisi* (Rome, 1926).

12. Arnaldo Fortini, *Nova Vita di San Francesco,* 4 vols. (Milan, 1926).

13. Gemma Fortini, "The Contribution of Arnaldo Fortini to Franciscan Studies," trans. Finbarr Conroy, in *Franciscan Studies,* vol. 43, annual 21 (St. Bonaventure, NY: Franciscan Institute, St. Bonaventure University, 1983), 263.

14. Arnaldo Fortini, *Francis of Assisi,* trans. Helen Moak (New York: Crossroad, 1992); taken from *Nova Vita di San Francesco* (Assisi: Tipografia Porziuncula, 1959).

15. Ibid., Gemma Fortini, "Contribution of Arnaldo Fortini," 261–278, 264.

16. Ibid., 262.

17. Ibid., 272.

18. Dalarun, *Misadventure,* 12.

CHAPTER ONE

1. From the writings of the thirteenth-century friar named Brother Elemosina, "Liber Historiarum," 78. Fra Elemosina, as he was known ("Fra" being an abbre-

viated Latin form for "brother"), with his brother Pietruccio, entered the Franciscan Order sometime after 1311. A deed of sale of their property, found in the archives of the Sacro Convento, dates to that time and carries their names.

2. Fortini has written about the belief that the world would end in *Assisi nel medioevo, leggende avventura, battaglie* (Rome, 1940), 2–5.

3. The controversy with Gregory VII, known as the Investiture Controversy, occurred between 1074 and 1076. Henry ascended to the throne as Holy Roman Emperor in 1085.

4. Henry's letter reads in its entirety:

Henry, king not through usurpation but through the holy ordination of God, to Hildebrand [the pope's family name], at present not pope but false monk. There is no grade in the church which you have omitted to make a partaker not of honor but of confusion, not of benediction but of malediction. To mention few out of many, you have trodden [bishops and priests] under foot like slaves ignorant of what their master is doing. You have won favor from the common herd by crushing them; you have looked upon all of them as knowing nothing, upon yourself solely, moreover, as knowing all things. This knowledge, however, you have used not for edification but for destruction. And we, indeed, have endured all this, being eager to guard the honor of the apostolic see; you, however, have understood our humility to be fear, and have not, accordingly, shunned to rise up against the royal power conferred upon us by God, daring to threaten to divest us of it. As if we had received our kingdom from you! As if the kingdom and the empire were in your and not in God's hand! By wiles, namely, which the profession of monk abhors, you have achieved money; by money, favor; by the sword, the throne of peace. And from the throne of peace you have disturbed peace, inasmuch as you have armed subjects against those in authority over them; inasmuch as you, who were not called, have taught that our bishops called of God are to be despised; on me also who, although unworthy to be among the anointed, have nevertheless been anointed to the kingdom, you have lain your hand; [I] who am subject to the judgment of God alone. For the true pope, Peter, also exclaims: "Fear God, honor the king." You, therefore, damned by this curse and by the judgment of all our bishops and by our own, descend and relinquish the apostolic chair which you have usurped. Let another ascend the throne of St. Peter, who shall not practice violence under the cloak of religion, but shall teach the sound doctrine of St. Peter. I, Henry, king by the grace of God, do say unto you, together with all our bishops: Descend, descend, to be damned throughout the ages.

"Henry IV: Letter to Gregory VII, Jan 24 1076," http://www.fordham.edu/halsall/source/henry4-to-g7a.html. Internet Medieval Source Book, a collection of public domain and copy-permitted texts related to medieval and Byzantine history (http://www.fordham.edu/halsall/sbook.html).

5. The pope's response in its entirety reads:

O St. Peter, chief of the apostles, incline to us, I beg, your holy ears, and hear me your servant whom you have nourished from infancy, and whom, until this day, you have freed from the hand of the wicked, who have hated and do hate me for my faithfulness to you. You, and my mistress the mother of God, and your brother St. Paul are witnesses for me among all the saints that your holy Roman church drew me to its helm against my will; that I had no thought of ascending your chair through force, and that I would rather have ended my life as a pilgrim than, by secular means, to have seized your throne for the sake of earthly glory. And therefore I believe it to be through your grace and not through my own deeds that it has pleased and does please you that the Christian people, who have been especially committed to you, should obey me. And especially to me, as your representative and by your favor, has the power been granted by God of binding and loosing in Heaven and on earth. On the strength of this belief therefore, for the honour and security of your church, in the name of Almighty God, Father, Son and Holy Ghost, I withdraw, through your power and authority, from Henry the king, son of Henry the emperor, who has risen against your church with unheard of insolence, the rule over the whole kingdom of the Germans and over Italy. And I absolve all Christians from the bonds of the oath which they have made or shall make to him; and I forbid any one to serve him as king. For it is fitting that he who strives to lessen the honor of your church should himself lose the honor which belongs to him. And since he has scorned to obey as a Christian, and has not returned to God whom he had deserted—holding intercourse with the excommunicated; practicing manifold iniquities; spurning my commands which, as you bear witness, I issued to him for his own salvation; separating himself from your church and striving to rend it—I bind him in your stead with the chain of the anathema. And, leaning on you, I so bind him that the people may know and have proof that you art Peter, and above your rock the Son of the living God has built His church, and the gates of Hell shall not prevail against it.

"Gregory VII: First Deposition and Banning of Henry IV (Feb 22, 1076)," http://www.fordham.edu/halsall/source/g7-ban1.html. Internet Medieval Source Book.

6. Cf. Fortini, *Francis of Assisi*, 141–142.

7. This is the Nicean Creed, an ecumenical statement of faith adopted by the Catholic Church. Originally written in Greek, the Latin version Francis would have memorized is as follows:

Credo in unum Deum,
Patrem omnipoténtem,
factórem cæli et terræ,
visibílium ómnium et invisibílium.
Et in unum Dóminum Iesum Christum,
Fílium Dei Unigénitum,
et ex Patre natum ante ómnia sæcula.
Deum de Deo, lumen de lúmine, Deum verum de Deo vero,
génitum, non factum, consubstantiálem Patri:
per quem ómnia facta sunt.
Qui propter nos hómines et propter nostram salútem
descéndit de cælis.
Et incarnátus est de Spíritu Sancto
ex María Vírgine, et homo factus est.
Crucifíxus étiam pro nobis sub Póntio Piláto;
passus, et sepúltus est,
et resurréxit tértia die, secúndum Scriptúras,
et ascéndit in cælum, sedet ad déxteram Patris.
Et íterum ventúrus est cum glória,
iudicáre vivos et mórtuos,
cuius regni non erit finis.
Et in Spíritum Sanctum, Dóminum et vivificántem:
qui ex Patre Filióque procédit.
Qui cum Patre et Fílio simul adorátur et conglorificátur:
qui locútus est per prophétas.
Et unam, sanctam, cathólicam et apostólicam Ecclésiam.
Confíteor unum baptísma in remissiónem peccatorum.
Et expecto resurrectionem mortuorum,
et vitam ventúri sæculi. Amen.

8. Regis J. Armstrong, J. A. Wayne Hellmann, and William J. Short, eds., *Francis of Assisi: Early Documents*, Thomas of Celano, *Remembrances* (also known as *Second Life*), and *The Legend of the Three Companions*; vol. II, 331 and 83, respectively. All citations from early sources are taken from this corpus (Armstrong et al.) unless otherwise noted.

More will be said of Thomas of Celano's *Remembrances* in the following chapter. The document titled *The Legend of the Three Companions* was written in 1246. Its authorship is unknown. But it is clearly written by one who knew Francis intimately at both the early and latter stages of his life. It is written with great sensitivity and perception and lends little-known details that are not found in other official legends. It was written as a result of a call for material rendered by the order's then–minister general, Crescentius of Iesi, who in

1244 "directed all the brothers to send him in writing whatever they could truly recall" about their life with Francis. It carries an introduction of sorts under the names of Leo, Angelo, and Rufino. The author of the body of the text, however, remains unresolved.

9. Bertran de Lananon, "*Us cavliers si iazia*," from Alfredo Cavaliere, *Cento lirche provenzali* (Bologna, 1938), 419.

10. Noted in the epigraph to this chapter.

11. For details related to the legend of Saint George, see Fortini's Italian work, *Nova Vita di San Francesco* 3:32–33.

12. From about A.D. 235 until the accession of Diocletian in 284, rapid turnover among emperors precludes tracking which emperor did what to whom.

13. From two codices, the Codex of the Museo dell'opera del Duomo of Perugia and the Codex of the Chiesa Collegiata di San Lorenzo of Spello.

14. Ibid. Perugia Codex. Also, "Il messale consultato da San Francesco." *San Francesco Patrono d'Italia* 58 (March 1978): 80–88.

15. Revelation 12:7ff.

16. *Mirror of Perfection* (Sabatier ed.), in Armstrong et al., *Francis of Assisi*, vol. III, 320.

17. "Writing in the second half of the twelfth century, Chrétien de Troyes was the inventor of Arthurian literature . . . drawing from material circulated by itinerant Breton minstrels and legitimized by Geoffrey of Monmouth's pseudo-historical Historia Regum Britanniae (History of the Kings of Britain, c. 1136–37). Chrétien fashioned a new form known today as courtly romance." Chrétien de Troyes, *Arthurian Romances*, trans. with intro. and notes by William W. Kibler (London: Penguin Books, 1991), 1. The mystique of King Arthur's Knights of the Round Table arose during this time as knights who earned the highest order of chivalry and thus sat at a table that had no head or foot. It represented equality of those who were seated.

18. Ibid., 211.

19. Ibid., 211–212.

20. Ibid., 262.

21. Ibid., 222–223.

CHAPTER TWO

1. The sources I highlight that explore Francis' pre-conversion life include Thomas of Celano's *First Life*, written in 1228; *The Versified Life of Francis*, written by the French poet Henri d'Avranches around 1230; *The Life of Francis*, written in 1234–1235 by Julien of Speyer; *The Legend of the Three Companions*, written

around 1247, and whose authorship is unknown (it is introduced by Francis' closest followers, brothers Leo, Rufino, and Angelo); and Bonaventure's *Major Life* (1260). I use Bonaventure primarily as a point of comparison, particularly regarding material he excluded from the official biography. He handled the formidable task of consolidating a great magnitude of material with sensitivity and control. Bonaventure was attempting to render a unified account of the saint, whose multiple and varied teachings were being (in some cases) isolated and championed by splintering factions within the order. He wrote an official biography to clarify Francis' mission and uphold the sanctity of his saint. However, by the time he wrote, the story had evolved and he polished it still further. His biography contains gaps and glosses over otherwise valuable historical material.

Some readers will question why I chose to use Henri d'Avranches and Julien of Speyer *along with* Thomas of Celano, since the first two depend upon the third and therefore add nothing new. Thomas of Celano—a friend and follower of Francis—was born of a noble family in the small town of Celano, in the region of Abruzzi south of Rome, between 1185 and 1190. Thomas was an academician who joined Francis in 1215 during the early stages of the order's development. Francis sent him to Germany around 1221, where Thomas assumed the role of local vicar to the friars in Worms, Cologne, Speyer, and environs. His *First Life* was the first biography of Francis to be written, having been commissioned by Pope Gregory IX on the occasion of Francis' canonization in 1228. Thomas' first legend was somewhat constrained by the pope's commission, but it relies heavily on Francis' own writings, his own personal experience of Francis, and direct testimony from those who knew Francis and lived with him. Thus the integrity of his narrative can be assumed because those whom Thomas consulted and who knew Francis would have been able to read his biography for error, before and after publication. The biography created a tempest, implicating Francis' family for the bad turn taken by their son in his youth. Francis' mother, Pica, was still living at the time and understandably took umbrage at the implications. The official reason rendered for commissioning, then, a second biography in 1246—requested not by the pope but by then–minister general of the order, Crescentius of Iesi—is the latter's desire to consolidate all the materials to date about Francis and rewrite one clear narrative. As will be seen, the story changed, sometimes dramatically, between Thomas's *First Life* and *Remembrances*. (The latter was later published under the title *Second Life*, included in the *Omnibus*. Since the writer cites primarily from the more recent Armstrong et al. edition, the title *Remembrances* is retained.) In any case, both the first legend and its rewrite were later ordered destroyed.

With Thomas's testimony I include references from the fourteen versified books written on the life of Francis by the then-well-known poet Henri d'Avranches in the 1230s. Henri d'Avranches was born in the French city of the same name between 1180 and 1200. His education reflects high standing in liter-ary and religious circles. During his lifetime, the art of putting prose to poetry was flourishing in the universities and the royal court, and Henri was known for his command of a wide scope of subject material. He had written versified versions of many lives before that of Francis. He put to verse the life of Saint Birinus (c. 650) and the life of Saint Oswald (c. 641). The archbishop of Canterbury, Stephen Langton, commissioned him to put into verse the life of his predecessor, Thomas Becket (1170). Henri was well schooled in the Greek and Roman classics and brought these elements to his narratives. His reputation and skill commanded the attention of Pope Gregory IX, Francis' great protagonist, who asked him to put Thomas of Celano's *First Life* to verse. The poet had little or no contact with Francis' followers at the time but came to know some of them, and this helped animate his pen. Upon completion (in 1239) he read all fourteen "books" before the papal court. In his lifetime Henri composed versified works for one pope (Gregory), two emperors, three kings, six archbishops, twelve bishops, and any number of abbots. Of the more than 160 poems that have survived, Henri is best known for his work on Francis.

The thrust of this work articulates the theme of his inner battle in clawing out of the abyss of lust and degradation to arise and dress himself in the armor of Jesus Christ. There is no historical evidence, of course, that Francis articu-lated his conviction with such polish. Yet reading it one gets a feel for the in-tense emotions during that wrenching and embattled moment. Inevitably this begs the question *Can a poet be a reliable source?* One cites Giotto's fresco cycle of the life of Saint Francis gracing the walls of the upper basilica of San Francesco. Giotto was the pivotal early fourteenth-century artist who is consid-ered to be the forefather of renaissance art. His twenty-eight scenes retell the life of Francis visually according to Bonaventure's details in his *Major Life* of Francis. Visual art was the only "book" the illiterate masses could read at the time. It could be argued in turn that what Giotto did with Bonaventure, Henri did with Thomas of Celano's *First Life*. His *Versified Life* could be considered the "Franciscan cycle" for the literati, based upon Thomas's life of Francis, painted with words. G. K. Chesterton notes, "He saw all things dramatically, so he was always dramatic. We have to assume throughout, needless to say, that he was a poet and can only be understood as a poet." Henri may have been less interested in Francis as a man or saint than in writing good poetry; his *Versified Life* may not add new information. But in a way that only an artist can do, Henri opens him up and takes his readers into the heart of a man.

It is proper, in turn, to add to this chorus of writers a German brother named Julien, who is measured, meticulous, and had no interest in embellishment or in advancing the cult of a saint. He resolved not to compose a hagiography for that reason. He wrote his biography of Francis in 1232 to 1235. Julien was born in the late 1100s (exact date unknown) in the German town of Speyer, an imperial city in the upper Rhine Valley. He was educated in Paris, in music, and won a place in the choir of the Royal Court chapel, where he was promoted to *magister cantor*. As a young man he had been delegated the responsibility of composing, directing, and organizing music for all religious and social functions at the French royal court.

It is known that he had joined the Friars Minor before October 1227, but the exact date is not known. His *Life of Francis* suggests he was present when Francis' remains were moved in 1230 from their temporary burial in San Giorgio to the newly built Basilica of San Francesco. Julien returned to Paris later that year and was integral in the organization and development of the Grand Couvent des Cordeliers, a "school of theology" for the order that ultimately attracted many learned doctors from the University of Paris. While doing this, he also composed and served as cantor for the proper singing of the Divine Office.

Julien's *Life of Francis*, therefore, was written in Paris. Though Julien never met Francis, he serves as an apt resource. He brought to his narrative, as one writer puts it, the "sensibilities of German Speyer and Paris, both urban centers typically at odds with the papacy." He depends upon Thomas of Celano's *First Life*, though he did not hesitate to depart from the approved text and move his narrative in other directions, making it succinct and to the point. Julien's text is shorter than Thomas', but, interestingly, the German master makes mention of Francis' stigmata more so than Thomas himself does. Another interesting point about Julien's account is that he makes no mention of Clare, her tonsure, her being asked advice from Francis, the dinner they shared at the Portiuncula, or Francis' retreating to San Damiano near the end of his life and writing the Canticle there. The only mention he makes of Clare is in his section about Francis' death, when the brothers carried his body to San Damiano, where she was living, before laying him to rest in Assisi.

2. From "Meeting of His Holiness Benedict XVI with the Priests of the Diocese of Albano, Swiss Hall at the Papal Summer Residence, Castel Gandolfo, Thursday, 31 August 2006." http://www.vatican.va/holy_father/benedict_xvi/ speeches/2006/august/documents/hf_ben-xvi_spe_20060831_sacerdoti-albano _en.html.

3. Thomas of Celano, *First Life*, in Armstrong et al., *Francis of Assisi Early Documents*, vol. I, 182–183.

4. Fortini, *Francis of Assisi*, 99.

5. *Three Companions*, in Armstrong et al., *Francis of Assisi*, vol. II, 68–69. The *Omnibus* translates the same section: "he strove to outdo the rest in the pomp and vainglory, in jokes, in strange doings, in idle and useless talk."

6. See note 1.

7. Thomas of Celano, *Remembrances*, in Armstrong et al., *Francis of Assisi*, vol. II, 242.

8. Bonaventure, *Major Life*, in Armstrong et al., *Francis of Assisi*, vol. II, 527.

9. Innocent III was thirty-seven.

10. This turbulent period in Assisi's history occurred during Francis' late teen years.

11. Etienne Baluze, "Vita Innocentii papae III," 1682, *Rerum Italicarum Scriptores*, vol. 3:492, per Fortini, *Francis of Assisi*, 120, n. 1.

12. Archivo della cattedrale di San Rufino, 8:57, per Fortini, *Francis of Assisi*, 167 ff.

13. Fortini, *Francis of Assisi*, 150.

14. Bonifazio, a thirteenth-century poet recounts details of the battle of Collestrada in his work *Eulista*, from the Italian historical archves 16:52; cf. Fortini, *Francis of Assisi*, 637, n. 60.

15. Ibid., Fortini, *Francis of Assisi*, 637, n. 60.

CHAPTER THREE

1. Fortini, *Francis of Assisi*, 162. Fortini derives detailed information about Francis' imprisonment from Luigi Bonazzi, *Storia di Perugia dalle origini al 1860*, 2 vols. (Perugia: Tip. di V. Santucci, 1875–1879), 261.

2. Cf. Fortini, *Francis of Assisi*, 639, n. 84ff.

3. Ibid., Archivo della cattedrale di San Rufino.

4. Ibid.

5. In the legends this young noble is called "Count Gentile," or a kind count.

6. Thomas of Celano, *First Life*, in Armstrong et al., *Francis of Assisi*, vol. I, 186.

7. Ibid.

8. *Three Companions*, in Armstrong et al., *Francis of Assisi*, vol. II, 70.

9. Ibid., 71.

10. Details of the dream include: "as he was falling to sleep, half awake, he heard someone asking him where he wanted to go. When Francis revealed to him his entire plan, the other said: 'What can do more good for you? The lord or the servant?' When [Francis] answered him: 'The lord,' he again said to him: 'Then why are you abandoning the lord for the servant, the patron for the client?' And Francis said: 'Lord, what would you have me to do?' 'Go back to your land,' he said, 'and what you are to do will be told to you.'" Ibid.; brackets in original.

11. Mariano Orza, *Gualtieri III di Brienne* (Napoli, 1940), 187ff.; cf. Fortini, *Francis of Assisi*, 189–190.

12. *Three Companions*, in Armstrong et al., *Francis of Assisi*, vol. II, 71–72.

13. Ibid., 72.

14. Thomas of Celano, *First Life*, in Armstrong et al., *Francis of Assisi*, vol. I, 188.

15. The document titled *The Legend of the Three Companions* was written in 1246. Its authorship is unknown. But it is clearly written by one who knew Francis intimately at both the early and latter stages of his life. It is written with great sensitivity and perception and lends little-known details that are not found in other official legends. It was written as a result of a call for material rendered by the order's then–minister general, Crescentius of Iesi, who in 1244 "directed all the brothers to send him in writing whatever they could truly recall" about their life with Francis. It carries an introduction of sorts under the names of Leo, Angelo, and Rufino. The author of the body of the text, however, remains unresolved.

16. The poet biographer Henri d'Avranches describes his confusion during this time: "He has a kind of debate with himself":

Do more things exist in the mind
than what he perceives with his senses?
Sense holds out feasts, allurements of love,
wealth and high honor and human approval—but cannot go any further.
Reason holds out life without end, delights in that City Above,
paradise joy, mysterious song, unspeakable light. . . .
One moment his mind is up in the air
and again it is down on the ground.

Henri d'Avranches, *Versified Life*, in Armstrong et al., *Francis of Assisi*, vol. I, 150 and 170.

17. Thomas of Celano, *First Life*, in Armstrong et al., *Francis of Assisi*, vol. I, 187.

18. Julien of Speyer, *Life of Francis*, in Armstrong et al., *Francis of Assisi*, vol. I, 372.

19. Thomas of Celano, *Remembrances*, in Armstrong et al., *Francis of Assisi*, vol. II, 248; emphasis in original.

20. *Testament of Saint Francis*, in Armstrong et al., *Francis of Assisi*, vol. I, 124. In Latin it reads: *Dominus ita dedit mihi fratri Francisco incipere faciendi poenitentiam: quia, cum essem in peccatis, nimis mihi videbatur amarum videre leprosos. Et ipse Dominus conduxit me inter illos et feci misericordiam cum illis. Et recedente me ab ipsis, id quod videbatur mihi amarum, conversum fuit mihi in dulcedinem animi et corporis; et postea parum steti et exivi de saeculo.* See http://www.franciscan-archive.org/index2.html.

21. Some have suggested this secret friend was Brother Elias, who joined Francis' order in 1213 and became minister general. He ultimately left the order in humiliation. If Brother Elias had been this loyal and beloved friend

who helped Francis convert, he made no mention of it during the years of controversy surrounding his role in the order before and after Francis' death.

CHAPTER FOUR

1. Gemma Fortini, "The Noble Family of St. Clare of Assisi," trans. Finbarr Conroy, *Franciscan Studies*, vol. 42, annual 20 (St. Bonaventure, NY: Franciscan Institute, St. Bonaventure University, 1982), 52.

2. Ibid., 48.

3. This information comes from the direct testimonies under oath as part of the investigation for Clare's canonization in *The Lady, Clare of Assisi: Early Documents*, rev. ed. and trans. Regis J. Armstrong (New York: New City Press, 2006). All references to documents from this corpus will be rendered in the notes as "Armstrong."

4. *Three Companions*, in Armstrong et al., *Francis of Assisi*, vol. II, 83.

5. This period would have followed the early stages of Francis' conversion when he was visiting caves with his unnamed special friend, whom the writer deems to have been Clare (see ch. 5, note 3). Their clandestine meetings after Francis' conversion suggest that they were not averse to the idea.

6. "Legend of St. Clare," in Armstrong, *Lady, Clare of Assisi*, 283.

7. *Mirror of Perfection*, in Armstrong et al., *Francis of Assisi*, vol. III, 362.

8. The archives in the Sacro Convento in Assisi contain many ancient documents that describe the pilgrimage to Rome, which was widely undertaken by Assisiani; cf. Fortini, *Francis of Assisi*, 641, n.12.

9. Thomas of Celano, *Remembrances*, in Armstrong et al., *Francis of Assisi*, vol. II, 247; *Three Companions*, in Armstrong et al., *Francis of Assisi*, vol. II, 73–74.

10. Bonaventure, *Major Life*, in Armstrong et al., *Francis of Assisi*, vol. II, 535.

11. Ibid., 562.

12. Ibid., 563; emphasis in original. Bonaventure locates this episode as occurring after his order had spurned him, near the end of his life.

13. Julien of Speyer, *Life of Saint Francis*, in Armstrong et al., *Francis of Assisi*, vol. I, 377.

14. D'Avranches, *Versified Life*, in Armstrong et al., *Francis of Assisi*, vol. I, 444.

CHAPTER FIVE

1. Thomas of Celano, *First Life*, in Armstrong et al., *Francis of Assisi*, vol. I, 189.

2. Ibid., *ut secum morari pro Domino pateretur*.

3. The sources do not identify this friend. Some have suggested it might have been Brother Elias, who joined Francis' order in 1213. This is unlikely. Later, when Elias was at odds with the order, he made no mention of this intimate connection to, influence over, and support of the young Francis during the early stages of his religious pining. Because of the intentional obscurity of the identity of this friend, as well as the period of Francis' life when this bond was forged, the writer believes it was Clare.

4. D'Avranches, *Versified Life*, in Armstrong et al., *Francis of Assisi*, vol. I, 162, 193.

5. Ibid.

6. *Three Companions*, in Armstrong et al., *Francis of Assisi*, vol. II, 78.

7. Fortini, *Francis of Assisi*, 221, trans. n. o.

8. Thomas of Celano, *First Life*, in Armstrong et al., *Francis of Assisi*, vol. I, 192.

9. *Three Companions*, in Armstrong et al., *Francis of Assisi*, vol. II, 79.

10. Ibid.

11. Ibid., 80; brackets in original.

12. Ibid.; emphasis in original.

CHAPTER SIX

1. Julien of Speyer, *Life of Francis*, in Armstrong et al., *Francis of Assisi*, vol. I, 194; cf. Bonaventure, *Major Life*, in Armstrong et al., *Francis of Assisi*, vol. II, 539.

2. D'Avranches, *Versified Life*, in Armstrong et al., *Francis of Assisi*, vol. I, 455.

3. Fortini, *Francis of Assisi*, 242 ff.

4. *Three Companions*, in Armstrong et al., *Francis of Assisi*, vol. II, 81.

5. Ibid.

6. Francis hadn't assumed a life of poverty in order to denounce wealth. He refused to condemn the wealthy, and once his order had blossomed, he demanded the same from his brothers.

7. Bonaventure, *Major Life*, in Armstrong et al., *Francis of Assisi*, vol. II, 589.

8. Julien of Speyer, *Life of Francis*, in Armstrong et al., *Francis of Assisi*, vol. I, 377.

9. *Three Companions*, in Armstrong et al., *Francis of Assisi*, vol. II, 83.

10. Julien of Speyer, *Life of Francis*, in Armstrong et al., *Francis of Assisi*, vol. I, 377.

11. "Testament of Saint Clare," in Armstrong, *Lady Clare of Assisi*, 60–61.

12. Thomas mentions an earlier follower about whom little is known. *First Life*, in Armstrong et al., *Francis of Assisi*, vol. I, 203.

13. They also read from Luke 9:3, "Take nothing for your journey"; and Matthew 16:24, "If any man will come after me, let him deny himself."

14. Fortini, *Francis of Assisi*, 276–277.

15. Tancredo was an influential member of Assisi's citizenry and, being fiercely devoted to the ideals of the *comune,* was a member of the governing consul that led the revolt of 1198.

16. Others, in name only, include Sabbatino, Morico, John of Capella, Philip the Long, John of Saint Constantia, Barbaro, Bernard Viridante, Silvestro, and Juniper.

17. Julien of Speyer, *Life of Francis,* in Armstrong et al., *Francis of Assisi,* vol. I, 380.

CHAPTER SEVEN

1. Fortini, *Francis of Assisi,* 208 ff.

2. According to the *Fioretti*:

It happened once that the friars were taking care of leprosy patients and sick people in a hospital. And a certain man was there who was seriously ill with leprosy. He was so impatient and irritable that everyone was sure he was possessed by an evil spirit. He attacked the friars who nursed him with horribly foul language and shot insults at them like arrows. What was worse he would also whip and wound them in various ways. Yet the most fearful and worst of all was that he would curse and blaspheme the Blessed Christ. No one could be found who could or would take care of him. The friars therefore decided to abandon that man completely.

Francis went to the sick man and rendered his standard greeting: "God give you peace, my dear brother."

The man answered, "What peace can I have from God, who has taken from me all peace and everything that is good, and has made me rotten and stinking?"

Francis said: "My dear son, be patient, because the weaknesses of the body are given to us in this world by God for the salvation of soul. So they are of great merit when they are borne patiently."

The sick man replied: "How can I bear patiently this constant pain that afflicts me day and night? Not only am I burned and crucified by my sickness, but I am sorely wronged by the friars whom you gave me to take care of me, because there is not one who serves me the way he should."

Francis said, "Dear son, I want to take care of you, since you are not satisfied with the others."

The sick man replied, "All right. But what more can you do for me than the others?"

Francis said, "I will do whatever you want."

The leprosy patient said, "I want you to wash me all over because I smell so bad that I cannot stand it myself."

Francis had water boiled with many sweet-scented herbs. He undressed the man with leprosy and began to wash him.

Fioretti, in *Omnibus*, 25, 1356–1357. (For details about this source, see ch. 9, note 14.)

3. Thomas of Celano, *First Life*, in Armstrong et al., *Francis of Assisi*, vol. I, 212; Julien of Speyer, *Life of Francis*, in Armstrong et al., *Francis of Assisi*, vol. I, 383.

4. An unknown writer in a codex in Perugia, from Annabale Mariotti. *Saggio di memorie istoriche civili ed ecclesiastiche della citta di Perugia e suo contado* (Perugia, 1806), 3:242; cf. Fortini, *Francis of Assisi*, 294ff. Trivium is the medieval name for grammar, rhetoric, and dialectic; quadrivium, for music, arithmetic, geometry, and astronomy.

5. Fortini, *Francis of Assisi*, 294ff.

6. Ibid., 295.

7. Thomas of Celano, *Remembrances*, in Armstrong et al., *Francis of Assisi*, vol. II, 254.

8. Bonaventure, *Major Life*, in *Omnibus*, vol. I, 651. Armstrong includes this version in a note, vol. II, 548.

9. Bonaventure, *Major Life*, in *Omnibus*, vol. I, 653.

10. Catharists and Waldensians similarly embraced poverty, as Francis did, but denied the authority of the Roman Church, asserting that Jesus conferred on every individual authority as a "priesthood" (from the New Testament, I Peter 2). The Cathars also upheld the notion that the divine spark within every human being was corrupted by the flesh, thus concluding the material world was evil. Waldensian conviction was not altogether inconsistent with that of Francis. However, when the movement's founder, Peter Waldo, solicited permission to preach from Church authorities, he was refused. Nevertheless, he continued to preach without permission. Waldensians and Catharists were both deemed heresies.

11. Bonaventure, *Major Life*, in *Omnibus*, vol. III:9, 652.

12. Ibid., vol. III:10, 653.

13. Julien of Speyer, *Life of Francis*, in Armtrong et al., *Francis of Assisi*, vol. I, 385.

CHAPTER EIGHT

1. The scene is depicted on the cover of this volume. It is an altarpiece, made in Nuremberg, Germany, in 1360, for Saint Claire Lournt (tempura and gold on oak panel).

2. "The Acts of the Process of Canonization of Clare of Assisi," in Armstrong, *Lady, Clare of Assisi*, 191.

3. The image on the book cover depicts that Palm Sunday with Francis waiting in the wings with a pair of scissors in his hand.

4. In 1201 Pope Innocent III issued a bull granting Benedictine sisters the rights to grant asylum and to offer protection against use of violence for those in their care.

5. "Legend of Saint Clare," in Armstrong, *Lady, Clare of Assisi*, 25.

6. New sources add more details about this dramatic event. These include *The Versified Legend of Saint Clare* (author unknown), written in 1254 shortly after Clare's death; and the *Legend of Saint Clare* (author also unknown), written as part of the canonization in 1255. All are found in the Armstrong, *Lady, Clare of Assisi* (see chapter 4, note 3.)

7. "Legend of Saint Clare," in Armstrong, *Lady, Clare of Assisi*, 5. I say "years" because, regarding San Damiano as noted by Thomas of Celano in his *First Life*, Francis "repaired it zealously within a short time. This blessed and holy place [is] where the glorious religion and most excellent Order of Poor Ladies [the Order of the Poor Clares] and holy virgins had its happy beginning about six years after the conversion of the blessed Francis and through that same man."

CHAPTER NINE

1. *Mirror of Perfection*, in Armstrong et al., *Francis of Assisi*, vol. III, 320.

2. *Legend of Perugia*, in *Omnibus*, 1043.

3. *Fioretti*, in Armstrong et al., *Francis of Assisi*, vol. III, 587.

4. Ibid., 583.

5. Ibid., 618.

6. "The Fourth Consideration: How, After the Imprinting of the Holy Stigmata, Saint Francis Left Mount Alverna and Returned to St. Mary's of the Angels," *Fioretti*, in *Omnibus*, 1458.

7. All three, along with Brother Angelo, stayed devoted to Francis throughout their lives and are buried near him in the Basilica of San Francesco in Assisi.

8. *Fioretti*, in Armstrong et al., *Francis of Assisi*, vol. III, 583.

9. Ibid., 621.

10. This wording is found in the *Omnibus*, 1376.

11. *Sed quando dicet tibi: tu es dampnatus, et tu secure respondeas: Apri la bocca, mo te caco! Fioretti*, in Armstrong et al., *Francis of Assisi*, 29.

12. *A Letter to Brother Leo*, in Armstrong et al., *Francis of Assisi*, vol. I, 122. The original autograph can be seen in the Cathedral of Santa Maria Assunta, in Spoleto.

13. *Mirror of Perfection*, in Armstrong et al., *Francis of Assisi*, vol. III, 333; emphasis in original.

14. The *Fioretti*: Originally published in Latin under the title *Actus-Fioretti*, it has more recently been called the *Fioretti*, or "Little Flowers." The writer did not know Francis' earliest companions, but his good friend, a brother named James of Massa, did know them. James of Massa had been quite close to brothers Masseo, Juniper, Giles, Simon, and Leo, and also to Clare. After the decree of 1266, when all legends had been ordered destroyed, a follow-up summons went out in 1276 soliciting additional material to supplement Bonaventure's biography. It was then, it is assumed, that Ugolino began scribbling the stories about Francis he had heard from James of Massa, who had heard them from the mouths of those "who knew him."

The *Fioretti* is controversial because it arose during a time when the order was splintering into divisions that still exist today, and some assert it is slanted in defense of one position. The strength of the book, however, is the other side of the same coin: the time of its writing. As noted, it was written after the decree of 1266 and was not therefore officially commissioned by a pope or officer of the Church. It is considered an independent source compiled by a sympathetic and diligent writer who understood the value of the great stories told by old friends like Leo. Ugolino's work introduces heretofore unpublished and unknown episodes about Francis. The book's weakness is its overblown and phantasmal interpretation of some events, as will be seen, which tends to undermine its believability. In any case, a careful and discriminating examination of it renders the astute reader nuggets of authenticity and simplicity about Francis and his friends that ring true. The epigraph reads: "This book contains certain little flowers, miracles, and inspiring stories of the glorious little poor man of Christ, Saint Francis, and some of his holy companions as revealed by their successors which were omitted in his biographies but which are also very useful and edifying."

15. *The Deeds of Blessed Francis and His Companions*, in Armstrong et al., *Francis of Assisi*, vol. III, 449–450. This is an early fourteenth-century manuscript noted in the appendix of the *Fioretti*.

16. "Canticle of Exhortation to Saint Clare and Her Sisters," in Armstrong, *Lady, Clare of Assisi*, 393.

17. "'Since it seems this way to you, it also seems that way to me,' he [Francis] responded. 'She has been enclosed for a long time in San Damiano and it will do her good to see the place of Saint Mary [the Portiuncula], where she was tonsured and became the spouse of Jesus Christ; and there we will eat together in the name of God.'" *Fioretti,* in Armstrong et al., *Francis of Assisi,* vol. III, 590.

18. I have been told by those in the Catholic religious community in Assisi that the idea of the cloister was less to keep the women in than to keep men out. Particularly in the Middle Ages, these communities of women could fall prey to brigands or intruders if they made their presence too public. Francis was very protective of Clare and assumed personal oversight of her cloister at San Damiano. She was frail in health, and he constantly exhorted her to take better care of herself. As for his hesitancy to have her come to the Portiuncula, one can only speculate. Women were forbidden there, generally, so he and his brothers broke protocol by allowing her to come. Beyond that, it is conceivable that he wanted to avoid possible temptations of a carnal nature.

CHAPTER TEN

1. Not all researchers concede that Francis made the trip at all. However, all the primary legends include the episode, and multiple other early and independent sources attest his presence there, including an Arab source.

2. Some say the Crusades included nine expeditions. Other skirmishes continued into the sixteenth century.

3. Chesterton, *Saint Francis of Assisi,* 136.

4. Fortini, *Francis of Assisi,* 121–122. He is citing documents from the Archivo del Sacro Convento.

5. Fortini, *Francis of Assisi,* 121–122.

6. A thirteenth-century Italian Franciscan and historian named Fra Salimbene (1221 to 1290) wrote an indispensable source for the history of Italy titled the *Cronica,* covering the period between 1168 and 1288. Salimbene describes his many travels and meetings with various celebrated personalities, and Jean de Brienne was numbered among them.

7. Green, *God's Fool,* 202.

8. Joseph François Michaud, *Bibliothéque des Croisades,* 4 vols. (Paris, 1829), bk. 12; cf. Fortini, *Francis of Assisi,* 400 ff.

9. Thomas of Celano, *Remembrances,* in Armstrong et al., *Francis of Assisi,* vol. II, 265; emphasis in original.

10. Bernardi Thesaurarii, *Liber de Acquisitione Terrae Sanctae ab an. 1095 ad an. Circiter 1230, gallice scriptus, tum in latinam linguam converses circ. 1320 a fr.*

Francisco Pipino, bononiensi Ord. Praed, in Rerum Italicarum Sciptores, 835; cf. Fortini, Francis of Assisi, 408.

11. The siege on Damietta was documented in detail by an unknown chronicler whose work was consolidated and published by Alberto Milioli, a third-order Franciscan born in central Italy in 1220, who knew Salimbene and shared historical notes with him. The description of the battle comes from Milioli's document Gesta obsidionis Damiatae; cf. Fortini, Francis of Assisi, 408 ff.

12. Fortini, Francis of Assisi, 408ff.

13. Attributed to the Muslim mystic Fakhr-al Farasi, who was his counselor; cf. Fortini, Francis of Assisi, 428, trans. n. o.

14. I draw upon sources including Thomas of Celano, First Life; Julien of Speyer, Life of Francis; Henri d'Avranches, Versified Life; and Fioretti, all in Armstrong et al., Francis of Assisi. To these I have added from Writings of Jacques de Vitry, in Armstrong et al., Francis of Assisi, vol. I, "Letter of 1220" and "History of the Orient,"580–585; an anonymous thirteenth-century account of the Fifth Crusade credited to the words of Brother Illuminato, who accompanied Francis to visit the sultan (Anonymous, "Saint Francis and the Sultan of Egypt, Verba di Frate Illiminato," Ms. Vaticano, Ottob. lat. 522); Girolamo Golubovich, Biblioteca bio-bibliografica della Terra Santa e dell'Oriente Francescano, vol. I (Quaracchi, 1906–1927); cf. Fortini, Francis of Assisi, 395 ff.; and a thirteenth-century chronicler named Ernoul, who wrote what is widely considered the most accurate of the several attempts to narrate the Crusades as a sequel to William of Tyre's twelfth-century narratives. Ernoul's document is called The Chronicle of Ernoul (1227–1229). These documents are found in Armstrong et al., Francis of Assisi, vol. I, 605–609. Fortini includes extensive notes on primary source material relating to this episode (Francis of Assisi, 635–639).

15. Chronicle of Ernoul, in Armstrong et al., Francis of Assisi, vol. I, 606.

16. Ibid., 606–607.

17. Ibid.

18. "Saint Francis and the Sultan of Egypt," Golubovich, Biblioteca, vol. I, 36–37.

19. See n. 14.

CHAPTER ELEVEN

1. The source for this information is a friar named Giordano of Giano in a thirteenth-century document called Analecta Franciscana.

2. Giordano of Giano, Chronica, 12. English trans. Placid Hermann, in XIIIth Century Chronicles (Chicago: Franciscan Herald Press, 1961), 1–77; cf. Fortini, Francis of Assisi, 436–47.

3. During Clare's lifetime the convent of women was called the Poor Ladies. After her death they assumed the name the Poor Clares.

4. *Assisi Compilation*, in Armstrong et al., *Francis of Assisi*, vol. II, 132–133. This is a thirteenth-century document comprised of anecdotal recollections of early followers of Francis self-described as "we who were with him." It was compiled between 1244 and 1260 as a result of the summons of minister general (in 1244) Cresentius of Iesi to collect as much material as possible about the life of Francis. The collection reflects at times contradictory accounts and tracks, if inadvertently, of the ongoing fracturing within the order after Francis' death.

5. *Mirror of Perfection*, in Armstrong et al., *Francis of Assisi*, vol. III, 287.

6. During the year 1221 Francis set about writing the first draft of the order's official rule, which was destined to be rejected. Ultimately a second version was rewritten in 1223, which eventually won papal confirmation.

7. "A Letter to a Minister," *The Writings of Francis of Assisi*, in Armstrong et al., *Francis of Assisi*, vol. I, 97–98.

8. Ibid., 97.

9. "The Final Rule of the Friars Minor" (1223), *Writings of Saint Francis*, in Armstrong et al., *Francis of Assisi*, vol. I, 103–104, states: "If any brother, at the instigation of the enemy, sins mortally in regard to those sins concerning which it has been decreed among the brothers to have recourse only to the provincial ministers, let him have recourse as quickly as possible and without delay. If these are priests, with a heart full of mercy, let them impose on him a penance; but, if the ministers are not priests, let them have it imposed by others who are priests of the Order, as in the sight of God appears to them more expedient. They must be careful not to be angry or disturbed at the sin of another, for anger and disturbance impede charity in themselves and in others."

10. He was buried at the Portiuncula. The inscription on his grave marker reads: "In the year of our Lord 1221, six days before the ides of March, Frate Pietro Catanio, who rests here, returned to the Lord."

11. Opinions vary as to how this came to pass. Some historians maintain Cardinal Ugolino appointed him, whereas others insist Francis himself appointed Elias, since he (like Peter of Catanio) was a man of law. Little else is clear about what else transpired at that chapter.

12. "The Words of Brother Conrad," *A Collection of Sayings of the Companions of Blessed Francis (Late 13th–Early 14th Century)*, in Armstrong et al., *Francis of Assisi*, vol. III, 127. (Conrad of Offida, 1237 to 1306, was a brother who was sympathetic to the *Zelanti*.)

13. Ibid., 128.

14. The previous rule, the "primitive rule," approved by Innocent III, hadn't established the brothers as an order, but merely governed them as an assemblage of religious men who had been granted approval to preach.

15. Matthew 10; 19:21; Luke 9:3; Matthew 16:24; and related passages.

16. *Mirror of Perfection*, in Armstrong et al., *Francis of Assisi*, vol. III, 288. The *Assisi Compilation* adds, "We who were with him when he wrote the Rule and almost all of other writings bear witness that he had many things written in the Rule and in his other writings, to which certain brothers, especially prelates, were opposed" (in Armstrong et al., *Francis of Assisi*, vol. II, 212).

17. Thomas of Celano, *First Life*, in Armstrong et al., *Francis of Assisi*, vol. I, 244.

18. *Omnibus*, vol. I, 707.

CHAPTER TWELVE

1. *Legend of Perugia, in Omnibus*, vol. II, 1058.

2. *Assisi Compilation*, in Armstrong et al., *Francis of* Assisi, vol. II, 212.

3. Julien of Speyer, *Life of Francis*, in Armstrong et al., *Francis of* Assisi,vol. I, 406. The Christmas Eve service at Greccio was the first documented account of a "manger scene."

4. "The Undated Writings," "At Compline / Antiphon: Holy Virgin Mary / Psalm," *Writings of Saint Francis*, in Armstrong et al., *Francis of* Assisi, vol. I, 140. The reading is excerpted.

5. Described in Arnaldo Capelli, "Le Malattie di San Francesco d'Assisi: Raccolta di Saggi," sponsored by Centro de Servizi Culturali in the province of Chieti (region of Abruzzo, Italy), 1983. The paper was presented at the Centro Culturale Aldo Moro at the Chieti Scalo on October 27, 1982.

6. Angelo Fiori and Nicolo Miani, "La Ricognizione Del Corpo di San Francesco, Il Rapporto dei due medici addetti all ricogniczione" (Assisi: Case Editrice Francescana, 1978), 55–57. I consulted as well with professore Padre Pasquale Magro, O.F.M., Conv., who was present in 1978 at the examination of Francis' mortal remains.

7. D'Avranches, *Versified Life*, in Armstrong et al., *Francis of* Assisi, vol. I, 510.

8. "The Second Consideration: How Saint Francis Spent His Time with His Companions on Mount Alverna," *Fioretti*, in *Omnibus*, vol. II, 1438.

9. *Legend of* Perugia, in *Omnibus*, vol. II, 1068.

10. Thomas of Celano, *First Life*, in Armstrong et al., *Francis of* Assisi, vol. I, 264. Henri writes:

So does Jesus' passion remain implanted in his heart,
So imprinted right through the marrow of his soul
That it cannot be hid, but must flood outwardly
And mark its likeness on his partnered flesh,

Becoming visible, as it were, through transparent limbs.
The five wounds of the Redeemer appear impressed
In their separate places.
D'Avranches, *Versified Life*, in Armstrong et al., *Francis of* Assisi, vol. I, 510.

11. Julien of Speyer, *Life of Francis*, in Armstrong et al., *Francis of* Assisi, vol. I, 410.

12. *Legend of Perugia*, in *Omnibus*, vol. II, 1070.

13. Gordon College, Orvieto, Italy, September 2007.

14. Another question that has been raised is why Francis' wounds—at least as they are depicted in art and described in the legends—appear on the palms of his hands when crucifixions nailed the metatarsal bones of the wrist. In his meditations Francis was picturing the wounds of Christ on the hands, not the wrists, regardless of the way the crucifixion actually happened. Byzantine crosses and other early representations of Christ depict Jesus' wounds through the palms. These images would have informed Francis' mental picture of Christ's suffering. Whatever Francis' meditations of the crucifixion might have been, he would have pictured the hand wounds upon the palms.

15. After La Verna, Francis "concealed it to the best of his ability." *Three Companions*, in Armstrong et al., *Francis of* Assisi, vol. II, 108.

16. *Legend of Perugia*, in *Omnibus*, vol. II, 1082.

17. *Legend of Perugia*, the *Mirror of Perfection*; the episode is also mentioned in the *Fioretti*.

18. Bonaventure and Henri d'Avranches.

19. Thomas of Celano, *Remembrances*, in Armstrong et al., *Francis of* Assisi, vol. II, 384 and 385; emphasis in original.

20. Afterward Francis would travel south to Rieti, to receive treatment for his eyes.

21. *Legend of Perugia*, in *Omnibus*, vol. II, 1023.

22. The Canticle as it was written in Umbrian, along with the author's English translation, appears in the appendix.

23. *Legend of Perugia*, in *Omnibus*, vol. II, 1021.

24. Canto I, 1–3:
La Gloria di colui che tutto muove
Per l'universo penetra; e risplende
In una parte piu e meno altrove

The glory of the All-Mover
Penetrates through the universe and reglows
In one part more and in another part less.

25. Francis says of the sun, quoted in the *Legend of Perugia*: "The sun is the most beautiful of all creatures because it is the one which, better than all the others, could be compared to God. At sunrise every person ought to praise God for having created this heavenly body which gives light to our eyes during the day; at evening, when night falls, everyone ought to praise God for that other creature, our brother fire, which enables our eyes to see clearly in the darkness. We are all like blind people, and through these two creatures God gives us light. Therefore, for these two creatures and for the others that serve us each day, we ought to praise their glorious Creator in a very special way." *Legend of Perugia*, in *Omnibus*, vol. II, 1022.

26. Interestingly, the Canticle makes no mention of animals.

CHAPTER THIRTEEN

1. *Fioretti*, in *Omnibus*, vol. II, 1344. Armstrong's version reads "holy words," vol. III, 599.

2. *Legend of Perugia*, in *Omnibus*, vol. II, 1026.

3. Ibid.

4. Ibid., 1027.

5. Ibid.

6. *Testament of Saint Francis*. Leo notes his reason for writing it, *Legend of Perugia*, in *Omnibus*, vol. II, 993–994.

7. Assisi had sovereignty over Nocera, and assuming Francis was going to die there, they deemed it safer for him to die outside of Assisi, and beyond the reach of Perugia.

8. Fortini, *Francis of Assisi*, 598–599. The encounter is depicted in Thomas of Celano's *Remembrances*, in Armstrong et al., *Francis of Assisi*, vol. II, 281.

9. *Mirror of Perfection*, in Armstrong et al., *Francis of Assisi*, vol. III, 370.

10. *Cucco* was an idiosyncratic term used in Assisi to denote someone stupid.

11. "*Bene veniat*" or "*Benvenga*" (singular) or "*Benvegnate*" (plural) is the Italian/Umbrian expression for "welcome."

12. *Legend of Perugia*, in *Omnibus*, vol. II, 1075.

13. Ibid., 1085.

14. The Romans called it *mostacciuolo*. It was made from almonds and sugar.

15. *Legend of Perugia*, in *Omnibus*, vol. II, 1082.

CHAPTER FOURTEEN

1. "A Letter on the Passing of Saint Francis, Attributed to Elias of Assisi," in Armstrong et al., *Francis of Assisi*, vol. II, 489. This is a reconstruction rendered

by a seventeenth-century Franciscan named William Spoelberch in a document titled *Speculum vitae b. Francisci et sociorum ejus II*. Oddly, given the significance of the occasion, the original document has never been found. We are left, to date, only with this reconstructed version.

2. Ibid., 489–490.

3. Only after Francis' death did the brothers have the opportunity to get a good look at his body. "Letter on the Passing of Saint Francis," in Armstrong et al., *Francis of Assisi*, vol. II, 489ff.

4. He is known to have once climbed on the roof of a building under construction that he had believed to belong to the order and started tearing the roof off. *Legend of Perugia*, in *Omnibus*, vol. II, 987.

5. Omer Englebert, *Saint Francis of Assisi*, trans. Eve Marie Cooper (Chicago: Franciscan Herald Press, 1965), 158–159.

6. Known then as the crypt.

7. In Latin the phrase reads "*magis tumultuose quam canonice.*"

8. Hence the branch of the order known as "the Conventuals." The controversy surrounding Elias's leadership of the order resulted in the division of the order into two—and later three—parties: the *Zelanti*, who upheld the strict observance of the rule, later named the Observants; and the Conventuals, who followed Brother Elias's model of cultural adaptation, education, and engagement (living in "convents"). The Capuchin, the third branch on today's Franciscan landscape, are stricter than the Observants and the Conventuals.

9. He was elected to the papacy in March 1227.

10. In Latin, *Inquisitores haereticae pravitatis*.

11. Gregory was opposed to torture. But his immediate successor, Innocent IV (and others who followed), employed it regularly in the attempt to root out heresy. Gregory was clearly a political player. At the same time, many deem him one of Christendom's most spiritual popes. During his papacy he canonized saints Elizabeth, Dominic de Guamán, Anthony of Padua, and, of course, Francis.

12. "Sentence of Deposition, Council of Lyons, June 1245," "Frederick II (r. 1215–1250): Dispute with the Church, 1245–1246," http://www.fordham.edu/halsall/source/1245FrederickII.html. Internet Medieval Source Book.

13. "The Encyclical letter *Eger cui levai*, c. 1246," "Frederick II (r. 1215–1250): Dispute with the Church, 1245–1246," http://www.fordham.edu/halsall/source/1245FrederickII.html. Internet Medieval Source Book.

14. In the nineteenth century, Pope Pius VI declared him "Blessed."

15. In addition to the introductory letter of the *Legend of the Three Companions*, Leo is credited with writing a life of Blessed Giles called *Aegidius of Assisi*. He is thought also to have collaborated on the biography of Clare that was written about 1257.

16. The remains of these four brothers were moved from the lower basilica to the area surrounding Francis' crypt in the 1930s.

17. Taken from a personal interview with Padre Pasquale Magro, March 2005.

18. *The Kinship of Saint Francis by Arnald of Sarrant*, in Armstrong et al., *Francis of Assisi*, vol. III, 680. Fortini's research concurs that the above-mentioned Chiara became a Poor Clare at the monastery of Sant' Angelo di Panzo (where Francis took Clare before San Damiano) and is listed in the archives among the abbesses. He confirms as well that the archives list Angelo and Francesco as being in residence at the Sacro Convento and, later, as guardians of San Damiano.

19. Leo writes about the circumstances of the composition of this Canticle in the *Legend of Perugia*, in *Omnibus*, vol. II, 1024–1025: "When he thought of [the sisters] his spirit was always moved to pity because he knew that from the beginning of their conversion they had led and were still leading an austere and poor life by free choice and out of necessity. He especially asked them to treat their bodies with discernment and discretion, and to use alms God would send them with joy and thanksgiving. He recommended that the healthy sisters bear patiently with the fatigue brought on by their care of the sick, and that the latter endure their sicknesses and their needs with patience."

20. Chiara Frugoni in a personal interview by e-mail, June 2007.

21. Pathology tests on her mortal remains to confirm her malady have not been undertaken, and there are no plans to do them. Her symptoms are consistent with bone tuberculosis as described in Edwin S. Wilson Jr. and Edward G. Whiting Jr., "Disseminated Tuberculosis of Bone," *California Medicine* 105, no. 4 (1966): 284–287.

22. Clare's mother moved to San Damiano immediately after Francis' death.

23. A quote from Sister Anastasia Chiara, a Poor Clare I visited at the cloister of the Basilica of Santa Chiara, explaining that the iron grill that separated us as we spoke was "a symbol of our separation from the world," November 28, 2006.

24. Thomas Merton, *The Wisdom of the Desert: Sayings from the Desert Fathers of the Fourth Century* (New York: New Directions, 1960), 9.

25. When the Franciscan martyrs were killed in Morocco in 1219, Clare wanted to go there. But Francis kept her cloistered. "She had to adapt to the ideals of chivalry," historian Simona Fanelli said in an interview (February 2007). "Francis spent his life outside the friary on his missions while Clare, the lady, stayed behind to organize the life of the sisters and also of the friars."

26. "First letter to Agnes of Prague" (1234), in Armstrong, *Lady, Clare of Assisi*, 43.

27. "Second letter" (1235), in ibid., 47.

28. "Third letter" (1238), in ibid., 50.

29. Agnes built a monastery for the Poor Clares in Prague and joined the order in 1236 along with seven other noblewomen. Clare sent five sisters from San Damiano to join them. Agnes died in March 1282 and was canonized in 1989.

30. Robinson, "St. Clare," in *Franciscan Essays*, Sabatier et al., 33.

31. Her rule pertained only to San Damiano and not to other convents. After Clare died it disappeared. In the early 1900s the abbess at Santa Chiara found it hidden inside an old habit of Clare's, thus animating new hope that more documents may yet be found.

32. "Legend of Saint Clare," in Armstrong, *Lady, Clare of Assisi*, 46.

33. "Notification of Death," in Armstrong, *Lady, Clare of Assisi, 135ff.*

34. Her sternum, left kneecap, some ribs, and other bones were missing, and researchers found other bones that were "not possible to be those of Saint Clare." No conclusive testing has been done to determine the nature of the bone malady that crippled her.

35. During the investigation for Clare's canonization, Lady Filippa recounted a dream Clare had had late in her life, which she described to the sisters:

> Lady Clare related how once, in a vision, she brought a bowl of hot water to Saint Francis along with a towel for drying his hands. She was climbing a very high stairway, but was going very quickly, almost as though she were going on level ground. When she reached Saint Francis, the saint bared his breast and said to the Lady Clare, "Come, take and drink." After she had sucked from it the saint admonished her to imbibe once again. After she did so what she had tasted was so sweet and delightful she in no way could describe it. After she imbibed, that nipple or opening from the breast from which the milk comes remained between the lips of blessed Clare. After she took what remained in her mouth in her hands, it seemed to her it was gold so clear and bright that everything was seen in it as in a mirror.

"The Acts of the Process of Canonization of Saint Clare," Third Witness, in Armstrong, *Lady, Clare of Assisi*, 29; see also the Sixth Witness, 13; and the Seventh Witness, 10. In Clare's *Testament* she mentions Francis by name eighteen times; she mentions "God," "the Lord," and the "Father," twenty-seven times.

CHAPTER FIFTEEN

1. *The Basilica of St. Francis in Assisi*, ed. Gianfranco Malafarina (Modena, Italy: Franco Cosimo Panini Editore Spa, 2005), 122.

2. Conversation with Padre Pasquale Magro, June 2007, at the Sacro Convento, Basilica of San Francesco, Assisi. The friar was referring to Giotto's image in the upper basilica of San Francesco depicting Francis shouldering the falling Basilica of St. John Lateran.

Glossary of Terms

* * * * * * * * * * * *

Abbot/Abbess: A friar or sister who is in charge of particular monastery.

Alemanni: A name given to Germanic peoples in the Middle Ages.

Basilica/Cathedral: *Basilica* was originally used to describe a Roman public building; the term has evolved to refer to a large and important church that has been given special ceremonial rites by the pope while retaining an aspect of public accessibility for architectural, artistic, or ecclesiastical purposes. A *cathedral*, on the other hand, is a Christian church that contains the seat of a bishop. It is intended for worship and serves as the bishop's seat, thus as the central church of a diocese.

Curia: The Roman Curia, taken from the Latin word that means "court," is the administrative counsel of the central governing body of the Roman Catholic Church. It is comprised of the pope and cardinals.

Divine Offices: Saint Benedict of Nursia (c. 480–543) is credited with creating a structure organization for the liturgy of offering prayers at various points of the day, including morning, at the third hour, the sixth, the ninth, the evening, and at "cock-crowing." The eight "Divine Hours," called the Divine Offices, are known by the following names:

Matins (during the night or predawn hours of the morning)

Lauds (at dawn)

Prime (First Hour = 6 A.M.)

Terce (Third Hour = 9 A.M.)

Sext (Sixth Hour = 12 noon)

None (Ninth Hour = 3 P.M.)

Vespers ("at the lighting of the lamps"—evening)

Compline (before retiring)

General Chapter: The gathering of all elected representatives of the order from all provinces to discuss business, make decisions, share fellowship, and set a course for the future.

Hagiography: An important literary genre in the early Christian church, providing historical information as well as inspirational stories and legends. (See below.)

Hospitaller: Also known as the *Knights Hospitaller*, an organization that began as an Amalfian hospital founded in Jerusalem in 1080 to provide care for poor and sick pilgrims to the Holy Land. After the conquest of Jerusalem in 1099 during the First Crusade, it became a Catholic military order under its own charter and took on the name Knights Hospitaller. The order was charged with the care and defense of pilgrims to the Holy Land.

Indulgence: In early Roman Catholic theology it was the full or partial remission of temporal punishment due to sins granted forgiveness by the church after the sinner had confessed and received absolution, or in some cases given money. Martin Luther's challenge of the abuses of indulgences ignited the sixteenth-century Reformation.

Legend: A book of record of the deeds of a saint; not intended to be a biography in the strict sense.

Mendicant (Latin mendicare, "to beg"): Members of religious orders in the Roman Catholic Church who take a vow of poverty renouncing personal and communal property. The term has evolved to describe those in the penitential movement who went from place to place to preach.

Minister General: The head of the order within each respective branch (Conventual, Observant, Capuchin).

Order of Friars Minor:

> Observant (OFM): The Observant branch strives to uphold the simple lifestyle modeled by Francis. They live in hermitages. Their tunics are brown. They shave.

> Conventual (OFM Conv): The Conventuals, in the Middle Ages, was a generic designation for Franciscans who lived in a stable house (*conventus* in Latin) and not in caves and hermitages. This branch encourages education and the building of universities. Their tunics are gray or black. They wear blue jeans outside the convent.

> Capuchin (OFM Cap): The Capuchin friars, which evolved in the sixteenth century, sought to return to and uphold the primitive way of life in solitude and penance as practiced by the founder of his order. They wear a brown tunic and usually have long beards.

> Order of Saint Clare of Assisi or "Clares" (OSC): The "Poor Clares," as they are also sometimes called, was a Franciscan Order founded by Clare (as the Order of Poor Ladies) to establish communities of women who wanted to embrace the penitential life as embraced by Francis.

> Third Order Franciscans (TOF): Also called the SFO—Secular Franciscan Order—was created in 1221 by Francis to accommodate brothers and sisters

of the penitential movement who wished to live by the order's convictions but were prevented from joining because of marriage or other ties.

Rule: The governing document of a religious order.

Sacro Convento: The friary, or living quarters, in Assisi connected to the Basilica of San Francesco.

Saracens: Another name for the Arab empire (Muslim) under the rule of the Umayyad and Abbadis dynasties.

Templars: Also known as Knights Templars, they were a medieval Christian military order prominent in the Crusades from the early 1100s until the early 1300s.

Tonsure: In the Roman Catholic Church the "first tonsure" (a symbolic cutting of hair about the size of a coin leaving a bare spot toward the back of the head) was, in medieval times, the rite of qualifying someone for the civil benefits then enjoyed by clerics, primarily the privilege to preach.

Selected Bibliography

· · · · · · · · · · · ·

Armstrong, Regis J., J. A. Wa7mann, and William J. Short, eds. *Francis, of Assisi: Early Documents*. 3 vols. New York: New City Press, 1999.

Bartoli, Marco. *Clare of Assisi*. Trans. Frances Teresa. Quincy, IL: Franciscan Press, 1993.

Brook, Rosalind B. *The Image of St. Francis: Responses to Sainthood in the Thirteenth Century*. New York: Cambridge University Press, 2006.

Chesterton, G. K. *Saint Francis of Assisi*. Garden City, NY: Doubleday/Image Books, 1951. (Originally published in 1924)

Cook, William R., ed. *The Art of the Franciscan Order in Italy*. Leiden, The Netherlands: Brill, 2005.

Cunningham, Lawrence S. *Francis of Assisi: Performing the Gospel Life*. Grand Rapids, MI: Erdmans, 2004.

Dalarun, Jacques. *The Misadventure of Francis of Assisi: Toward a Historical Use of the Franciscan Legends*. Trans. Edward Hagman. Saint Bonaventure, NY: Franciscan Institute Publications, 2002.

de Troyes, Chrétien. *Arthurian Romances*. New York: Penguin Books, 1991.

Englebert, Omer. *St. Francis of Assisi: A Biography*. Trans. Eve Marie Cooper. Chicago: Franciscan Herald Press, 1965.

Fortini, Arnaldo. *Francis of Assisi: A Translation of Nova Vita di San Francesco*. Trans. Helen Moak. New York: Crossroad, 1992.

Frugoni, Chiara. *Francis of Assisi: A Life*. New York: Continuum, 1998.

Frugoni, Chiara. *Una solitudine abitata: Chiara d'Assisi*. Roma: Laterza, 2006.

Green, Julien. *God's Fool: The Life and Times of Francis of Assisi*. Trans. Peter Heinegg. San Francisco: Harper & Row, 1985.

Habig, Marion A., ed. *St. Francis of Assisi Writings and Early Biographies: English Omnibus of the Sources for the Life of St. Francis*. 2 vols. Trans. Raphael Brown, Benen Fahy, Placid Hermann, Paul Oligny, Nest de Robeck, Leo Sherley-Price. Quincy, IL: Franciscan Press, 1991.

Jörgensen, Johannes. *Saint Francis of Assisi: A Biography*. Garden City, NY: Doubleday/Image, 1955.

Ledoux, Claire Marie. *Clare of Assisi*. Trans. Colette Joly Dees. Cincinnati: St. Anthony Messenger Press, 2003.

LeGoff, Jacques. *Saint Francis of Assisi*. Trans. Christine Rhone. New York: Routledge, 2003.

Magro, Pasquale M.*Guida completa all'iconografia della Basilica di San Francesco in Assisi*. Assisi, Italy: Case Editrice Francescana, 1996.

Magro, Pasquale M. *Il simbolismo cristiano della chiesa-reliquiario di San Francesco in Assisi*. Assisi, Italy: Casa Editrece Francescana, 1993.

Merton, Thomas, trans. *The Wisdom of the Desert: Sayings from the Desert Fathers of the Fourth Century*. New York: New Directions, 1960.

Moorman, John R. H. *Saint Francis of Assisi*. Chicago: Franciscan Herald Press, 1963.

Sabatier, Paul. *The Road to Assisi: The Essential Biography of St. Francis*. Intro. and annot. Jon Sweeney. Brewster, MA: Paraclete Press, 1989.

Spoto, Donald. *Reluctant Saint: The Life of Francis of Assisi*. New York: Penguin, 2002.

Index

. . . .